In praise of
Man to Man, Dad to Dad

"I highly recommend this faith-filled, insightful, and practical book of essays to inspire fathers to embrace their holy vocation, so essential for the new evangelization of our culture."

— Most Reverend Kevin C. Rhoades, Bishop of Fort Wayne-South Bend and Chair of the USCCB Committee on Laity, Marriage, Family Life, and Youth.

"Our world needs a renewal of fatherhood. This book will help you become the best version of yourself as a father! I hope it inspires you the way it has inspired me."

— Matthew Kelly, founder of the Dynamic Catholic Institute, author of more than a dozen books, including *The One Thing: Passing Faith onto Children*, *Building Better Families: A Practical Guide to Raising Amazing Children*, and *Rediscover Catholicism: A Spiritual Guide to Living with Purpose and Passion*; husband and father of two

"This is a book for every Catholic man, especially husbands and fathers. Clear, practical, and profound, each and every chapter is sure to inspire, challenge, equip, and empower. Highly recommended."

— Scott Hahn, professor of Scripture and theology, Franciscan University of Steubenville; author of *A Father Who Keeps His Promises: God's Covenant Love in Scripture*, husband, father of six, and grandfather of eight

"We live in a culture that does little to uphold or promote authentic masculinity. Brian Caulfield has done Christian men a great service in compiling the wisdom of virtuous fathers who have forgone the advice of the world and have chosen holiness instead."

— Matt Fradd, Catholic apologist and speaker, creator of The Man Talk DVD, husband and father of three

"This is a book that is filled with profound insights and advice from some of the best men and dads. They speak from their own experiences as the men of faith they are. I encourage you to read this book and become the man and dad that God created you to be!"

— Fr. Larry Richards, founder and president of The Reason for our Hope Foundation; author of *Be a Man! Becoming the Man God Created You to Be*

"*Man to Man, Dad to Dad* should find a place in every Catholic home. Here is frank and honest advice about everything—from discipline to religious upbringing to even, yes, sex—all presented with clarity and charity, from some of the most engaging and thoughtful Catholic fathers writing today. Seek it out, read it, and then share it with a Dad you know!"

— Deacon Greg Kandra, Diocese of Brooklyn; Executive Editor, *ONE Magazine*; creator and editor of the popular blog The Deacon's Bench; resides in Forest Hills, New York with his wife, Siobhain

"Both a challenge and a hope, this book throws down the gauntlet, challenging all Catholic men looking to be better husbands and fathers."

— Sean McCarney, host of Just A Catholic Dad podcast, children's liturgist, Salisbury City Catholic Pastoral Council Communications Officer; resides in the U.K. with his wife and six-year-old daughter

MAN TO MAN, DAD TO DAD

MAN TO MAN, DAD TO DAD

Catholic Faith and Fatherhood

Edited by Brian Caulfield

Foreword by Cardinal Timothy M. Dolan

Pauline
BOOKS & MEDIA

Boston

Library of Congress Cataloging-in-Publication Data

Man to man, dad to dad : Catholic faith and fatherhood / edited by Brian
Caulfield ; foreword by Cardinal Timothy M. Dolan.
    pages cm
  ISBN-13: 978-0-8198-4918-2
  ISBN-10: 0-8198-4918-9
  1. Catholic men--Religious life. 2. Fathers--Religious life. 3. Fatherhood
--Religious aspects--Catholic Church. 4. Families--Religious aspects--
Catholic Church. I. Caulfield, Brian, editor of compilation.
  BX2352.5.M326 2013
  248.8'421088282--dc23
                            2012048235

The Scripture quotations contained herein are from the *New Revised
Standard Version Bible: Catholic Edition,* copyright © 1989, 1993, Division of
Christian Education of the National Council of the Churches of Christ in
the United States of America. Used by permission. All rights reserved.

Cover design by Rosana Usselmann

Cover photo: istockphoto.com/ © peter zelei

Published by Pauline Books & Media, 50 Saint Pauls Avenue, Boston, MA
02130-3491

Printed in U.S.A

www.pauline.org

Pauline Books & Media is the publishing house of the Daughters of St.
Paul, an international congregation of women religious serving the Church
with the communications media.

2 3 4 5 6 7 8 9   17 16 15 14 13

To my wife, Maria, the love of my life,
who has made me the father that I am,
and to St. Joseph, the model for all men.

Contents

Foreword

I was very blessed to grow up in a family where my mother and father's love for each other, rooted in their sacrament of Marriage, was constantly on display, as was their love for me and my brothers and sisters.

My dad's love for us was very clear, particularly in so many little things that he did. For example, Dad would come home every day at about 5 P.M. In the summer, he would get out of his car, with his shirt clinging to him, since it was hot and he was sweaty and tired. I'm sure that all he wanted was to kiss my mother, change his clothes, drink a cold beer, eat supper, and relax. But I would stand outside my house with my baseball and glove and ask, "Dad, will you play catch with me?"

And, despite his fatigue, he and I would play catch for a few minutes. It wasn't a big deal. It was just a little, insignificant thing. But it sticks with me to this day. My dad knew the importance of small acts of love—and so does God, our Father.

That example of love is at the heart of this wonderful book about fatherhood by Brian Caulfield. Brian does excellent work as the editor of an attractive website, "Fathers for Good," and he brings his wisdom and experience to this book. He has gathered other men from across the nation to share their own expertise and experience, to help men shoulder the responsibilities and blessing of the vocation of fatherhood.

There is no doubt that this kind of book is urgently needed in our nation and in our Church. The absence of fathers from the lives of children has already reached crisis proportions and has led to all kinds of personal and social problems. Our culture and media seem to have lost any sense of the impact that a father can have on the lives of his children and routinely deride or ridicule "traditional" fathers.

The antidote to that cultural decline can be found in the essays in this book. They address compelling, urgent needs in the lives of fathers and children—strengthening and preserving marriages, disciplining children with love, learning sportsmanship, and keeping kids Catholic. They wrestle with hard problems, such as pornography, balancing work and family, and moral relativism. They offer beautiful insights into the teachings of the Church on marriage and sexuality, particularly Pope John Paul II's Theology of the Body. This is a very rich book, filled with practical advice that will resonate with men and appeal to their better natures and aspirations.

My dad taught me how to love, through the small acts of kindness and sacrifice that he made for me and my brothers and sisters. Readers of this book will encounter that same kind of love of good fathers and will learn how to be better fathers themselves. I heartily encourage all fathers—and mothers too—to explore the book's gifts and be enriched in their vocations.

TIMOTHY MICHAEL CARDINAL DOLAN

Archbishop of New York

Introduction

Dads in Deed

Brian Caulfield

"Congratulations, you're a father!"

Hearing those words for the first time is a transforming moment in any man's life, and for many of us it marked our passage into a new world of love, joy, and responsibility. Holding that little life in your hands for the first time, and seeing some small reflection of yourself in the infant's eyes, is a life-changing experience that you will always carry within. Wow, Dad, look what you've done!

By the time the little one wraps a hand around your finger and holds on for dear life, you know you're in this for keeps. For as long as you live you will be a father, and not a day will go by when you will not in some way labor for the benefit of your child. Long after he or she has gone out into the world, you will still want to know where your child is and how he or she is doing in life.

The joys of fatherhood are many. Yet today, there exist many questions and uncertainties about the role of a father in the life of his children and family. What does it mean to be a man and a father in today's world when some even question the need for a father? The slippers-and-pipe image of the all-knowing dad from the 1950s has long since passed—perhaps for the better—but have we developed any workable image to take its place? Indeed, we have few guides in this new world of easy divorce, widespread single motherhood, and women choosing children alone through sperm donors and in-vitro fertilization or adoption. We men may wonder if our paternal role is valued at all in the law or the culture. Some may feel that their instinct to protect and provide for a family is negated by women who have better educations and higher paying jobs. In the wake of such seismic changes in relations between the sexes, in what way can we men be valued for our unique masculine strengths and virtues?

How exactly does our Catholic faith fit into this picture? When we enter a church and see—on an average Sunday in the average parish—more women than men in the pews, we may even wonder if our Church values our presence and participation.

Yet the last thing a man wants to do in this situation is to feel sorry for himself. That would be self-defeating, and tears in your beer don't make it taste any better. Yes, perhaps you deserve a medal for navigating the crooked paths of our culture and emerging with your masculinity and sanity mostly intact. But for all your efforts at balancing family and work, diapers and deadlines, manhood and the feminine mystique, the most you are likely to get for a job well done is more work.

But maybe that's enough. For men willing to invest the effort, there are opportunities today for blazing a new path. Much has been written about the "Greatest Generation" from the World War II era, which our fathers or grandfathers lived through. The men of that time are presented as unreachable icons called to higher duties, who gave or risked their lives to make the world safe for freedom. Many were heroes, with larger-than-life exploits. Yet just because we can't repeat that glorious past doesn't mean we should count ourselves out. Today, by our actions and decisions, we can make another Greatest Generation. Under very different family, social, and political conditions, in an America that is challenged in different ways by situations within our borders and by enemies outside, we can be the heroes of our own era.

Although we live in a culture that tends not to prize heroism, and men have few worldly incentives to develop the chivalrous virtues of physical strength and moral restraint, we have a chance to stand against the tide and be true men of virtue. We can be quietly but insistently countercultural in the way we live and relate to others, particularly in our duties as husband and father.

In a society that is wedded to the escape hatch of divorce, we can honor our wedding vows, "for better, for worse . . . till death do us part." In a day when so many use abortion as a backup for contraception, we can cherish every human life as we respect all women, especially our wives. As science puts forth a "brave new world" of reproductive options that are used by even decent, well-intentioned couples, we can embrace the marriage act as the natural and exclusive means to bring new life into the world, knowing that every soul rests in the loving hands of God, not the confines of a petri dish.

As editor of the website FathersforGood.org, I hear from many men who are quietly yet heroically living a life according to conscience, guided by the natural law and the teaching of the Catholic Church. Even if they have not lived perfect lives, these men understand the dual meaning of the term "Fathers for Good." First, once a man has a child, he is a father for good—there is no giving back the gift or commitment that comes with responsibilities. Second, every man, amid his own sin and weakness, deep down wants to be a good father. He wants to offer something of lasting value to his child that only a father can give. He knows that despite many negative portrayals in popular media and culture, there is a great dignity in the role of father.

Despite our best efforts, these are still difficult days for men and for fathers. Our identity and duties have been in flux for decades, and it is time for us to start building something new and better from the shifting sands of our culture. It's time to build the next Greatest Generation. If you're a man who has faith even the size of a mustard seed, there is a path for your marriage and your fatherhood that leads to the greatest satisfaction a person can have in this world—the grace and accomplishment of finding your vocation. For true fatherhood is a call from God the Father. This book is designed to help you locate that path and take those first steps along the way the Father has made for you to be a dad not just in name but in deed. Let us embrace the adventure.

1

The Prodigal Son Meets the Forgiving Father

Mike Aquilina

It is often said that newborns don't come with instruction manuals, and no one feels this lack of direction more deeply than a first-time father. Where is he to look for guidance in a culture that gives conflicting messages about masculinity and fatherhood? Is he to be the strong, silent type, a distant authority figure to his child? Or should he be a dad who is in touch with his feelings and comfortable with emotion?

Mothers have numerous *What to Expect* books to guide them from pregnancy through the toddler years. While many men take to fatherhood naturally, others start off somewhat confused about both their role and their duties. Yet there is a lot of wisdom in a place where many of us would not think to look: the Bible. In the Scriptures we find some basic parenting advice that's reliable and authoritative, as well as divinely inspired! For centuries, Jesus, Mary, and Joseph—the Holy Family—have served as a model for every family on earth, with love, generosity, and sacrifice at the heart of their home life.

Our biblical resource may not have the detail and precision of user manuals for a flat-screen TV or a gas grill, but most of us never pull those manuals out of the shrink-wrap anyway. Our Lord knew that about male nature in advance. So he gave us his parenting advice in stories that should make us think, and then pray, and then take on the discipline of doing things we'd prefer not to do. Yes, it can be painful to move out of our comfort zone and become a "biblical dad," but the payoff is well worth it.

The parables of Jesus, in which he holds up earthly fathers as an image of God, offer a very practical model of fatherhood. For example, in his parable of the wealthy landowner, we encounter a dad who includes his son in his work and shows confidence in him: "He had . . . a beloved son. Finally he sent him to [the tenants], saying, 'They will respect my son'" (Mk 12:6). We, too, should show our kids trust and confidence, letting them work with us whenever possible.

But Jesus' masterpiece on parenting is certainly his parable of the Prodigal Son (Lk 15:11–32).

The father in this story is trusting and forgiving, even to a fault by earthly standards. Indeed, he seems to go beyond any reasonable limit when he grants his younger son an advance on his inheritance. The ungrateful youth promptly leaves for "a distant country," where he squanders his share on "dissolute living."

Funny how fast money vanishes. The son goes broke and gets a job feeding pigs, which inspires in him a deep desire to be back in the comfortable home of his father. He soon plans his return and rehearses an apology: "Father, I have sinned against heaven and before you; I am no longer worthy to be called your son; treat me like one of your hired hands." How many times he must have repeated those words on the long journey home from the "distant country."

The father spots his son as he approaches. Does he wait at the doorway with his arms crossed and a knowing smirk on his face, conjuring up many variations of the line "I told you so"?

No.

"But while [the son] was still far off, his father saw him and was filled with compassion; he ran and put his arms around him and kissed him."

There's a lot we can learn from books about parenting. There's a lot more we can learn by watching good parents in action. But we can learn still more—so much more—by reading this parable, praying about it, and striving to live by it.

With six children, half of them now grown to adulthood, I have some experience with the issues raised by the parable. I know firsthand how difficult it is to deny oneself the pleasure of saying, "I told you so." I can tell you how hard it is to meet your child halfway on an apology, so the kid can save face. But maybe I don't have to tell you. Maybe you already know from your own experience as a father. Yet we need to put ourselves into the parable and take the role first of the son, and then of the father, and see what Jesus is telling us.

We have to be prepared to forgive often, because we're here on earth in a communion of clumsy saints. Our kids aren't the only ones who go around breaking rules and breaking vases. In our own ways, you and I do, too; and when we do, we ache for forgiveness, understanding—the compassion of the father in the parable. And we feel the pain when someone denies us forgiveness. Imagine how our children, who are dependent on us for so much, feel when we withhold forgiveness and make them feel smaller than they are.

We need not trust someone in order to forgive. The father of a delinquent child, or an addicted child, or a compulsively lying child, may have no reason to trust. But he still has every reason to forgive with compassion. Forgiveness is a beginning. We can defer our trust for many years, but we must not delay forgiveness or put conditions on it.

Sometimes we hold such anger toward our children that we feel a deep need to hear an apology. So we ask for one. But then the apology's not good enough. They didn't say the things we wanted them to say, the way we wanted them to be said. When it comes to our own grievances, we can become as fussy as a grammarian. Rules and more rules.

But that's all wrong. We cannot make someone else sorry. We can't change others. But, with God's grace, we can change ourselves. We can move from grievance to forgiveness, and we can make that movement again and again—maybe seventy times seven times, as Jesus instructs us (cf. Mt 18:22). We can learn to do this. And we must.

We learn our fathering from God our Father, who has given life to the parable of the Prodigal Son in the sacrament of Confession. There, the Father does not demand perfect penitence, just a sign of sorrow and the movement homeward. He's willing to work with any gesture. I'm reminded of the scene in Disney's *Aladdin* in which the genie wants to save the boy's life, but Aladdin is unconscious and can't command his own rescue. So the genie lifts the boy's head up, lets it fall back down, and says: "I'll take that as a yes."

God knows better than to trust us too soon, but he's eager to work with the little bit of sorrow we show. He'll take that as a yes. We should imitate him in our family life.

I think there is no more powerful witness to Christian living than a home where this dynamic of forgiveness is at work.

As fathers, we need to model forgiveness and forbearance. I find it easier if I have regular reminders that I'm also on the receiving end of those gifts. Thus I try to end every night with an examination of conscience and an Act of Contrition. And I go to Confession regularly. The best spiritual writers recommend that we go at least once a month. In our family, we make an appointment with a priest and, together as a family, each of us goes to Confession. If the kids grow up with the practice, they are less fearful of it, especially if they see that mom and dad need to kneel before the Lord, too.

Through regular Confession, we're much more likely to be forgiving at home, because we're much more likely to remember how much *we ourselves* depend on a forgiving Father. If we pray as Jesus taught us to pray, we've already entered into a bargain of sorts: "Forgive us our trespasses as we forgive those who trespass against us" (cf. Lk 11:4). In case we missed that message, Jesus said it again: "Forgive, and you will be forgiven" (Lk 6:37). And again: "He who is forgiven little, loves little" (cf. Lk 7:47).

This doesn't mean we have to be pushovers. Jesus left room for us to correct our children: "Be on your guard! If another disciple sins, you must rebuke the offender, and if there is repentance, you must forgive. And if the same person sins against you seven times a day, and turns back to you seven times and says, 'I repent,' you must forgive" (Lk 17:3–4). What's good for a brother is good for a son or daughter. We may rebuke, correct, and discipline our children, but always with an attitude of love and forgiveness.

Jesus even gave us the model for forgiving kids who seem clueless about their wrongdoing: "Father, forgive them; for they do not know what they are doing" (Lk 23:34). Those were among his last words, and he used them to plead for those who had hung him on the Cross and were, at that very moment, gambling for his clothing.

So, if you read only one book on being a father, let it be St. Luke's Gospel. If you read only one chapter, let it be Chapter 15 about the prodigal son and the forgiving father. It's the only foolproof guide to parenting. I know. I've tested it on the fallible father I know best.

2

St. Joseph: A Man's Man

RICK SARKISIAN

Do you have a role model, the man you'd most like to be like? Our culture gives us some questionable types to emulate. There's the alpha male with his macho "my-way-or-the-highway" swagger who grabs the girl. Or the pretty boy whom girls swoon over. Then there's the overly sensitive, soft male who avoids conflict and can't seem to decide even the simplest things in life.

They all may have their place in the world, but do you know who really gets my attention? The one man chosen by God to raise his Son: St. Joseph. The more I consider who Joseph was and *is* as Patron of Fathers, the more I'm convinced that he is the ultimate earthly example of a *real* man. He is a mix of the best qualities of every style of manhood. He was a strong carpenter who worked with his hands, a decisive leader who took Mary and Jesus out of danger, and a gentleman with "soft skills" who listened and sacrificed for the sake of his bride. Joseph's authentic manhood was the result of knowing that true power comes from utter reliance on God and that doing God's will is the most important mission in life.

Here are three ideas we can use right now to model St. Joseph's authentic manhood and gentle leadership to bring new vitality into our marriages and give our children tools that will last a lifetime.

Seek interior freedom

Ask anyone what he *really* wants out of life, and you're likely to hear the word "happiness." Yet there is no true happiness without love, and no love without a deep sense of interior freedom. After all, for love to be true, it must be freely given. In what appears to be a paradox, the Catholic Christian can only find true freedom through a trusting dependence on God—surrendering himself each day to divine providence and entrusting all of his needs to God. This is vastly different from the "autonomous self" that modern psychology often holds up as an ideal. The core value in today's culture tells us to "be your own man" and "do it your way." Yet true freedom is being a man of God and doing things *his* way—not as a slave before a master, but as a beloved son before a just father. We can experience within our hearts, minds, and souls what St. Paul calls the "freedom of the sons of God" (see Rom 8:21) by giving ourselves to the Father. As we do this, we become beloved sons with Jesus. This is true freedom—the freedom from sin and guilt that allows us to become real men of God.

Because we were created for love, we can only find happiness in loving and being loved. Teaching this truth to our children and embracing it as men is profoundly life-changing. Yet the kind of "love" promoted in today's culture is grounded in selfishness, based on getting rather than giving. That's why there are so many broken hearts and broken marriages. Real love and happiness occur only when spouses freely surrender themselves, giving themselves unconditionally to one another. It begins with acceptance of ourselves (including our limitations) and our spouses (including their limitations), and deciding to love them without end. This type of acceptance is the next step on the journey to authentic manhood.

In this context, think of what St. Joseph went through. When he found Mary was pregnant, he didn't condemn her, and he was "unwilling to expose her to public disgrace" (Mt 1:19). He sought to protect her from the harsh punishment of the Jewish law. God opened his heart, so that when the angel told him in a dream that Mary was pregnant by the Holy Spirit, he was free to respond in love and take her into his home.

Accept ourselves, accept suffering, accept others

The path of acceptance begins with accepting ourselves, particularly our weaknesses and flaws. It is a path paved with a desire to let Christ act in the daily events and circumstances of our lives.

Yet to reach authentic manhood we must travel the way of suffering, following Christ in accepting and embracing difficulties. These difficulties may be the result of our troubled past (regrets, guilt, emotional injury), or troubling circumstances of the present (job, finances, failure, death of loved ones). Suffering is an unavoidable part of life, and the worst thing we can do is try to avoid it at all cost, and so fail to grow.

This is a difficult message to accept in a culture that sees no sense in suffering and offers a pill or a self-help remedy for every kind of pain. Yet in a Christian perspective, suffering is not meaningless and can transform us for the better. We seem to understand this when we talk about sports—no pain, no gain. Yet we lose sight of the value of suffering when it comes to daily life. Christ suffered the ultimate pain—rejection by his own people and a humiliating death on a Cross. To be his follower, we should accept the lesser pain in our own lives. After all, heaven is the ultimate goal line.

So we have a choice: accept and actually embrace suffering—or fear suffering and reject it. By seeking to understand Christ's sufferings and how to accept our own when they come, we have the profound opportunity to teach our children about them—to show them that life's events are a call to grow and change. When good things happen, we respond with gratitude. When bad things happen, they are opportunities for personal growth and transformation. In Romans 5:3–4, St. Paul tells us that suffering produces perseverance, and perseverance character, and character hope. I believe there is no greater way of hoping in God than to entrust everything in my life—including my suffering—to him!

The journey of acceptance also requires that we accept other people, including the suffering caused by others. But before we can do that, we need to accept ourselves. When we fail to accept others, I believe it is often because we do not accept who we are. In essence, there is a battle within us that all too often puts us at war with others, forcing us to choose between forgiveness and resentment—between forgiving the faults and offenses of others, and hanging on to them because it gives us a false sense of power and control.

How did St. Joseph suffer? Imagine being told by an angel to get up and take your wife and child on a long, difficult journey because the king seeks to kill the baby. In all his trials, Joseph was the ultimate strong, silent type. Not a word of his is recorded in the Bible, yet he is remembered for his sure, decisive, and obedient action. He knew who he was before God; he accepted suffering as he accepted the people God gave him to love.

Live in the present moment

The only time I have is the present moment. How can I make the most of it? One key is to know that God is present in my life here and now, and that each moment is an opportunity to move closer to him or farther away. Each moment matters!

If we are constantly reliving the events of our past, we bump up against the harsh reality that we are powerless to change anything. Likewise, if we are fond of dreaming ahead, we realize that we have no control over what will come. Real peace and fulfillment are found here and now, as we seek God in the present moment. I believe Joseph demonstrated this attention to the present moment, and we are called to demonstrate this "now-ness" in our marriages and families.

While living in the present moment, we can rely on a spiritual GPS, what I call the "Divine Guidance System"—a kind of navigational aid for understanding God's will and purpose each day. We are guided by his word in Scripture, by the inspiration of the Holy Spirit within us, and by the events and circumstances of our lives.

Every event is a gift from God. Every moment is a call from God. He is present in everything that happens to us and wants to guide us in our daily lives.

Joseph certainly understood this, as he lived with true interior freedom while following God's call to live as the husband of Mary and the chosen father of Jesus. He knew about Jesus' divine origin, yet still accepted the momentous role of being his earthly father. He came to understand that Jesus must be about his "Father's business" (see Lk 2:49), yet he still expected a son's love and obedience. Joseph could not measure up to the divinity of Jesus or the Immaculate Conception of Mary, yet he still served as the masculine head of the family. He must have been a man of consummate confidence, with an unshakable strength of character, yet also one of simple humility, who sought God's will and carried it out with conviction. Living each moment with God's grace, Joseph experienced great interior freedom, even though he lived through difficult times.

We can know that kind of freedom, too, as we see each moment as an opportunity to protect, equip, guide, and teach our children, as well as to grow into holy men.

Starting right now, begin the practice of seeking interior freedom, accepting suffering—our own and others'—and living in the present moment. Then build on this solid foundation as you share these essential tools with your family. What an incredible gift you'll give them! And you'll be transformed in the process.

3

Balancing Work and Home Life: Insights from the Experts

BRIAN CAULFIELD

My father was a good man who worked hard during the week and had small weekend jobs to make ends meet for our family. He made time to do fun things with me and my two brothers on Saturdays, but during the week, he came home tired, ate dinner, watched TV while he read the newspaper, and left homework help, school projects, bath time, and bedtime to my stay-at-home mom. That was the 1960s. Things have changed for the average father today, who is expected to do a whole lot more at home, even as he may face more stress at work.

Adding to the equation is the fact that most wives now work outside the home, so some division of labor for family life must be worked out, which can become a source of conflict between spouses.

It is small wonder, then, that finding a balance between work life and home life ranks near the top of polls about challenges facing men today. While my father could engross himself in professional life as my mother kept the home fires burning, studies today show that within intact families, men are more involved in the daily routine of the household and the lives of their children. Yet the new normal for fathers is still being worked out. There can be a lot of uncertainty and stress as they struggle with demands at work in a weak and competitive economy, and seek to do the right thing at home, helping their wives with housework and child care.

It's a historic moment in many ways, an opportunity for dads to step up, seize the day, and make heroic efforts and sacrifices for their families. As men, we are more wired for hunting down prey than earning our daily bread by sitting at a desk all day. Yet today, unless we seek them out, there are fewer jobs and recreational opportunities for men to exhibit their physical strength and skills. However, all is not lost. The different challenges today offer men the chance to move out of their comfort zone as they blaze new paths and hunt down different prey. How we fathers deal with the new challenges of our own era will determine the kind of world our children and grandchildren will inherit.

In his book *Soft Patriarchs, New Men: How Christianity Shapes Fathers and Husbands*, W. Bradford Wilcox, a sociology professor at the University of Virginia, documents the rise of a new "servant leadership" image for fathers who embrace the demands of domestic life. Popular especially among evangelical Christians, the image is based more on the example of Jesus, who gave his life so that others may live, than on the warrior-kings of the Old Testament. Calling the modern Christian man a "soft patriarch," Wilcox shows how this new model of leadership is especially suited for our information and service economy, and the new dynamics of marriage and family life. Men can still fulfill that instinct for leadership—a trait most women value in them—yet they do this not so much by ruling as by dying to self so others may thrive within family life. Most of all, they do everything they can to build a happy marriage, avoid divorce, and stay engaged with their children. Based on Scripture, all of these themes should be familiar to Catholic husbands and fathers.

However, there is a lingering misunderstanding in our culture about male leadership or headship, let alone the word "patriarch." St. Paul's instructions in his Letter to the Ephesians has gotten a bad rap in recent decades because he advises that wives should be subordinate to their husbands as they are to the Lord (see Eph 5:22). When this passage comes up at Mass, there is even an option for the reader to leave out that sentence. "Subordinate" or "obedient" can sound foreign to the modern American mind, which is raised on individual rights and personal fulfillment. Yet, as Blessed John Paul II has written, what St. Paul has in mind is not a master-slave relationship, or even a king-subject one. St. Paul frames his points by talking first about the "mutual submission" of husband and wife, so when he says that the man serves as the "head," he compares this role to Christ as the head of his Bride, the Church. Before any husband thinks he is following the Bible by dominating his wife, he should read the rest of the passage in Ephesians:

> Husbands, love your wives, just as Christ loved the church and gave himself up for her, in order to make her holy . . . In the same way, husbands should love their wives as they do their own bodies. (Eph 5:25–28)

This "servant leadership"—to sacrifice and die for the beloved, just as Christ died for us—should apply to a man's decisions about work and home life.

Randy Hain, author of *The Catholic Briefcase: Tools for Integrating Faith and Work*, has faced head-on the challenges of work life and home life and made some difficult decisions. For many years, he chased the American dream of money and hard-driving success, yet he realized that he was missing some of the better things in life—time with his wife and involvement with his children. He made the tough choice of stepping off the fast track and recalibrating his priorities to put the needs of his family first. Today, he is the managing partner of an executive search firm in Atlanta and maintains a website to help men grow in their Catholic faith while reaching a balance in their professional and family lives.

A man should strive to support his family, though luxuries are not obligatory, Hain writes. But he insists that this duty must be met in the context of a much deeper *vocation*—a call from God—that comes with marriage and children. That call is to help your wife and children to get to heaven. If your work is an obstacle to the love and time you owe your family, God may be calling you to look for another job, Hain says.

He poses a tough question for dads today: "Is your job serving your family, or is your family serving your job?"

In an interview with me for the website Fathers for Good, he outlined a five-point plan for men:

1. Make family dinner a priority.
2. Turn off cell phone and other technology during family time.
3. Attend as many school and sports activities as possible.
4. Keep romance in your marriage with date nights and open affection.
5. Put God first—prayer and devotion set the tone and goals for a father and his family.

There were a number of interesting online comments to the posting of this interview that showed that men are seeking to address the problem in positive ways.

Talking about the tension between work time and family time, one reader noted: "That is a constant problem. It can also be a source of perpetual guilt, because if you are working, your family needs you at home. If you are at home, you aren't doing as much as you could/should to provide for them."

A computer programmer expressed the anxiety most men have of missing opportunities for advancement at work and even losing their jobs if they take too much family time.

He wrote: "I've found a good balance between work and home life. However, this means sacrificing some evenings and sleepless nights to finish a project. . . . The market is fragile, so my recommendation is to keep your firm family-first footing but tread lightly in expanding your rights with your employer."

One father stressed the need to support the foundational family relationship of husband and wife, and not let distractions come between them. He wrote, "Having a weekly date night (or lunch or breakfast) has been one of the most important parts of keeping our marriage on the right track. You will never regret this commitment."

Another father who has made sacrifices at work for the sake of his family said that things have worked out well, "I've changed jobs twice for the sake of my family, and I've never regretted it. My work is still meaningful and my family life is strong, because God is the first priority."

Let's face it, men, establishing a workable balance between your obligations at work and with family is not easy. It may be the most difficult task you will encounter in your married life. Men are good at immersing themselves at work. This is an especially attractive option if you get praise and pay raises at work, and headaches and demands at home. But don't fall into the workaholic trap.

The bottom line is that no one else can set this balance or solve your unique problems. You must take time for deep thought, communication with your wife, consideration for your children, and an evaluation of your position at work and your goals for career and income. The first step is to be aware that there needs to be a balance, and that it will definitely take hard work and great sacrifice. But men are made for that. Pray for guidance, keep your balance, and get going! The rewards will go far beyond your bank account.

4

Five Steps for Disciplining Kids

RAY GUARENDI

When it comes to discipline, dads can be caught in the middle. Our instincts often tell us to be strong and consistent authority figures—the tough-love types—but the culture discourages assertive masculine virtue, and nearly any sign of disciplinary action by men is looked upon as excessive. So too often we fathers stand in the background and leave the disciplining to Mom. Don't do it, Dad. Just as your kids need you in their lives for school, sports, and social skills, they need you in the all-important area of discipline.

Here is a basic five-point outline for being a disciplining, and disciplined, dad. Go over these with your wife so you can work together for the welfare of your children.

1. God made you their parents for a reason

As a licensed psychologist, radio talk show host, and speaker at numerous conferences, I am involved full-time in promoting good marriage and child-rearing practices. In addition, my wife and I have adopted ten children over the years. So I have heard about or personally dealt with just about every problem a family can run into.

Yet when parents approach me looking for that one insight that will solve their crisis, I don't give them some magic formula. Rather, I try to draw out from them the commonsense wisdom most parents have regarding their kids. In fact, I wrote a book on the topic called *You're a Better Parent than You Think!* With an overwhelming majority of parents, this is true. Father and Mother *do* know best. Yet a whole industry of child "experts" and "advisers" has spent the last half-century convincing parents that they really don't know much of anything and that someone else is better qualified to raise their kids.

Nonsense.

Yet given this state of affairs, much of what I do professionally is an attempt to give Mom and Dad the confidence and the tools to use their common sense and their unique relationship with their kids to do a decent job at what God has given them to do. Sometimes that attempt is a hard sell, and one of the most difficult areas is discipline. Okay, I agree that the old image of Dad standing over a quivering kid with a belt is not the kind of discipline we're looking for. But things have gone so far to the other extreme that too many parents are afraid to even look at their kids the wrong way for fear of injuring their delicate self-esteem.

Thus, when I tell parents to apply strong, consistent, and loving discipline, they are doubtful. They can't see how love and discipline go together, so I have to explain further.

2. Discipline is love in action

Lots of people think love is nurture and affection and support, and it is. But the other side is discipline. Discipline and love are on the same continuum of care for your child. It is incredibly *unloving* not to discipline your child. The simple reason: if you do not discipline your child, the world will. You do not want the world to discipline your child. The world is not a gentle place. The world does not view mitigating circumstances. By and large, the world does not love your child as you do.

So if you don't discipline, for whatever the reason—because you're tired, because you don't want to play the heavy, because you want your child to like you, or because your child is "superior" and exempt from discipline in your mind—you are setting him or her up to be disciplined by the world: a judge, a police officer, a parole officer, a landlord, an employer, an army sergeant.

Discipline without love is harsh and can be abusive, while love without discipline can be just as damaging. The damage is only delayed; it may take place years from now, but without discipline your child will get hurt. It's only a matter of time until this teen or adult who never grew up because of a lack of discipline presses against the boundaries that the world has set, and there will be trouble.

3. Discipline is action, not words

The great masquerade of discipline is words. Parents think they're strict because they yell loudly. They think they're great disciplinarians because they are "on a child," watching, waiting to deploy words of correction.

No. Words are weak. Generally, the only time when words are effective is when those words have been backed up in the past with action, and now action is no longer necessary.

For example, many of our own parents, or maybe grandparents, had "the look." They had only to set their stare in our direction and we knew that we'd best behave. This is especially true for fathers—we need to have a "look" so that our kids will not want to find out what lies behind it, because they know that you are willing to back it up with action. Depending on your child's age, this could include taking away a toy, unplugging the TV or digital device, canceling a sleepover, or suspending weekend privileges. Whatever the punishment, your child will feel a twinge of regret and hopefully a sense of remorse.

4. Perseverance

Consistency is critical, but there's another word that is just as important: perseverance. You will hear parents say, "I've tried everything with this child and nothing works, so I gave up. What could I do?"

Well, they could have tried harder. After two weeks, four weeks, six months, they just stopped whatever method of discipline they had started. In doing so, they sent a message to their child—just wait me out and you'll get what you want. In some way that parent is saying that love—which must take the form of discipline at times—only lasts so long.

I ask parents if they have negative qualities or behaviors that they've struggled with not just for months, but for five, ten, even fifteen years, for example, talking about people behind their back, losing your temper, procrastinating, saying petty things that set your spouse off. All parents agree that they do, of course, have bad habits that are hard to break. We all do. Then I'll point out that they've been trying for years to improve, yet they expect their kids to suddenly change after four weeks of reprimands and time-outs. It's not going to happen. You need to be persistent in discipline—again and again—even when you're tired, even if you think you've said it for the last time, even if you've decided to give up on your kid and consign him to the outer edges of humanity.

You must love enough never to give up on your seemingly incorrigible child. He will internalize your persistence, and one day when the chips are down, and it looks like all is lost, he will draw upon your persistence to overcome his own selfishness and weakness. Hopefully, you will be alive to witness it.

5. If you have authority, you discipline less

Authority is different from anger, or frustration, or even earnestness and seriousness. Authority is the perception by the child that Mom or Dad—preferably Mom and Dad together—mean what they say. Authority is the image that a loving parent can convey that basically says, "I love you without limits. However, when I am called to discipline with confidence and resolve as a parent, I will do so."

From a very early age, if a child perceives that a parent has this kind of authority, and that a parent is willing to act to enforce consequences, limits, and expectations for behavior, then the parent will need to discipline far less. Dads, take note. When you don't have that authority, when you are known to your child as someone who does not follow up words with action, then you will always be chasing your child through the paths of discipline and never quite catching up—sometimes overreacting and alienating your child, sometimes stopping and giving up, but always losing a vital grip on a proper father-child relationship

Now, believe me, no parent is perfect. Maybe we've already made a few mistakes in failing to discipline our kids. Yet the first step in exercising proper discipline is recognizing that it is important not only for the peace of your home, but also for the welfare and adult life of your children. Ultimately, you want them to listen because they respect you, and to respect you because they love you. It all starts with the recognition on your part that discipline is a high—yet challenging—form of love. Saying no and backing it up with action is often the best way to affirm your child.

You can do it, Dad.

5

Good Sports for Kids

GERALD KORSON

How do sports work out in your house? Does your kids' involvement keep you and your wife shuttling from field to court on weekends and dominate dinnertime during the week? Or do you manage to keep team sports in perspective, encouraging the positive values of good sportsmanship and pursuit of excellence while not letting athletics take over your family?

How you answer these questions—and you could add other activities such as ballet and music—will determine in large part the focus of your family's time and attention, and the priorities you express to your children. If your family is like

mine, you are constantly struggling to maintain balance
between sports and other worthy pursuits, and often doubting
your own wisdom.

Sports are an inescapable part of the American landscape,
virtually inseparable from our national culture. Each year, the
final games for both professional football and baseball draw
more than 100 million viewers around the world. In communities across the country, recreational leagues for all ages
abound in sports ranging from softball and soccer, to roller
derby and ultimate Frisbee.

According to the American Academy of Pediatrics, more
than 30 million children participate in sports each year in the
United States, and three-fourths of all U.S. households with
school-age children have at least one child who plays orga-
nized sports. From the world of professional sports to the
simplest of pickup games in our backyards or public parks,
sports are in our collective bloodstream.

That can be a good thing, too. It's easy to see how playing
sports can benefit children's well-being and development. The
exercise required by athletic competition strengthens their
bodies, improves their stamina, and may even extend their
lives. It refines motor skills, hand-eye coordination, and even
practical skills in mathematics (as with figuring out walk-strike-
out ratios and batting averages) and decision-making (to steal
or not to steal a base).

Then there are the less tangible ways in which sports can
help in moral character development. Athletics teach the values of teamwork, fairness, sportsmanship, and discipline, and
the importance of physical and mental preparation. Even

watching or attending sports events provides opportunities for learning these truths as well as for bonding as a family.

You should also be sure to include recreational sports in family time on weekends and vacations. Activities such as hiking, biking, camping, climbing hills, jogging, and backyard baseball, soccer, and volleyball can form lifelong bonds of fun and friendship within your family. These activities show kids that there is life apart from TV and video games and can keep them from becoming couch potatoes or screen addicts. This all means, Dad, that you should keep in shape yourself and set an example for your kids with healthy eating habits and exercise.

Children are not likely to take these life lessons to heart automatically, however. They are confronted with too many competing messages in what can often become a trash-talking, winning-is-everything sports culture. Positive values must be carefully taught and modeled by adults—particularly by parents. Our action and decisions send a strong message. If we make sure our kids get to soccer practice yet let them slide on completing homework, a lesson is learned, but not the right one.

Here are just a few of the key themes that my wife and I try to impress upon our own children.

Win or lose with grace. The opening theme to *ABC's Wide World of Sports* popularized the expression "the thrill of victory and the agony of defeat," complete with video of an unfortunate skier taking a brutal tumble down a mountainside. Both winning and losing are inherent in any competition, and our children must learn to deal with both outcomes.

Our son Mark was the quarterback for a sixth-grade football team that had considerable raw talent yet managed to lose every game. In the season finale, Mark threw a nice touchdown in the first half and mounted several impressive drives, but his potential game-winning pass into the end zone in the final seconds was batted away.

Mark took the loss hard—too hard. As he left the field, the opposing head coach stopped him to offer congratulations for an excellent game. Expressionless and silent, Mark stared ahead and kept walking.

Later that day, after the initial sting of the loss began to fade, I gently advised my son that he should have responded more positively to the coach's comments. It is as important to accept consolation from the winners as it is to act graciously in victory when the shoe is on the other foot.

But how often do we dads (and moms!) send that message? Maybe not as often as we think. Sadly, too many parents fail to model good sportsmanship. They cast aspersions upon referees, often failing to give the benefit of the doubt to officials who are trained in the rules and much closer to the action. Referees and umpires do make mistakes, but rarely is it helpful for spectators to hurl insults and catcalls in their direction. Following this example, our children may chime in with disrespectful behavior of their own.

Our daughter Adrienne was a certified soccer official at the age of sixteen and endured harsh treatment from fans, players, and coaches alike—at fifth- and sixth-grade matches, no less. The experience made her more aware of the difficulty of the referee's role and the respect they deserve from both participants and spectators.

Try to do your best. There's wisdom in the Cub Scout motto, "Do your best." To do one's best is all any parent can ask of a child, and the most any child should ask of himself.

Our children's elementary school competes in a citywide track meet with other Catholic schools each year, and one year two of our daughters decided to participate. Sophia entered the high jump and placed sixth. Adrienne, already in the back of the pack, knocked down the third barrier in the hurdles and politely stopped to reset it before continuing on to the finish line.

When he played youth-league baseball, our son Michael was neither a power hitter nor a base-stealing threat. But because he was tall for his age, he had a spacious strike zone that favored opposing pitchers. Fortunately, adolescent hurlers have notoriously terrible control, and Michael was content to let the bat rest on his shoulder. The result: a pretty good on-base percentage, but one due almost entirely to walks and being hit by pitches.

I taught Raymond to play tennis, and within a few short years he was beating me consistently. Although he never quite found a permanent spot on the first team varsity, he played hard in every match. Adrienne, starting goalkeeper and captain of her soccer team, arguably has enjoyed the most athletic success of all.

My wife and I take pride in each of their efforts. We seek a delicate balance in encouraging each child to strive for excellence without placing them under undue pressure. While we celebrate their successes, we emphasize that winning or losing is secondary to the satisfaction of knowing, in the common parlance of sports, that they "left it all out on the field" by utilizing their God-given talents to the maximum degree.

Keep things in perspective. One of the challenges that every parent faces is how to give each child the individual attention that he or she needs. Although this does not necessarily mean offering each child equal amounts of your personal time, most children readily take note whenever the activities and interests of one sibling seem to consume more of our time and attention.

Sports is one area that easily gives rise to this imbalance. Adrienne plays soccer year-round as she moves from the high school season to the travel leagues to the summer camps and conditioning—and her parents' time and attention move with her. For the children who are not as involved in athletics, it can all appear as one giant obsession. And perhaps, at times, it is. Do we, as parents, follow our children's sports schedules more intently than, say, their academic progress or their artistic development? Do we somehow convey the impression that athletic success is our most valued achievement?

Or are we, to some degree, vicariously living our own unfulfilled dreams of success in sports? I have to admit that a great amount of pride wells up in me as I bask in my kids' achievements. A juvenile competitiveness sneaks up on me when I tell neighbors about my child's win and inquire how their kids are doing. Yet I must guard against thinking that my offspring's success can add to my stature.

As crucial as it is to ensure that all our children receive the measure of love, attention, and affirmation they need in all their interests, sporting and otherwise, it is just as vital that we understand that sports are, after all, only games. When viewing or participating in athletic competitions takes an unhealthy precedence over family activities, school, health, and especially our relationship with God, it is time to step back and reassess our priorities. For starters, Sunday games that conflict with Mass attendance should be avoided at all costs. Yet we all know of leagues—maybe the one in our community—that schedule Sunday games which conflict with Mass obligations. And parents too often fail to object.

As Catholics, the highlight of our weekend must not be our kid's sports league or even the big game on TV. It must be our participation in the Eucharist at Sunday Mass, our worship of God, who bestows whatever athletic abilities our families possess and the capacity to appreciate the joys and lessons of healthy competition.

6

A Father's Vital Presence

Deacon Harold Burke-Sivers

My parents were divorced during my junior year in college and the only home I had ever known was sold. When my brother picked me up at the airport after I arrived from school that year, I asked him, "Where do we live now?" Driving to a new home in a new city with a broken family was a heart-wrenching experience. When young people ask me what it's like being a child of divorce, I tell them that marriage can be a cross, yet divorce is when the parents lay down the cross and the kids pick it up.

A few years later, when I informed my father that I was joining a Benedictine religious community, he was not just disappointed with my decision—he was downright angry. His comments went something like this: "You're going to do what? You are the first person in our family to go to college. I spent all that money sending you to one of the best universities in the country. You studied economics and business, and instead of making something of yourself, you're going to waste your life in that monastery living with a bunch of men? What is wrong with you?" From that day, our relationship was strained for a long time, even after I withdrew from the Benedictines and got married.

Sadly, my story is not unusual. Though the overall rate of divorce has leveled off nationwide, it is still far too prevalent. Too many fathers are abandoning their responsibilities or have been divorced by their wives against their will under no-fault divorce laws, and they struggle to keep connected to their kids. There is no question that we are in a fatherhood crisis where many men have completely abdicated or been legally barred from exercising moral and spiritual authority in the home. Instead of recognizing Christ within the sometimes monotonous rhythm of family life; instead of serving our wives and children with tenderness, love, and mercy; instead of working hard at deepening and strengthening our faith life, we allow ourselves to be shaped and influenced by the culture. We too often replace the fullness of self-donating love with self-seeking pursuits that never satisfy the heart.

These factors have brought about a perfect storm within family life, in which fathers are allowed and even encouraged to physically, emotionally, or spiritually abandon their wives and children.

With no fathers to model faith-filled leadership and God-centered authority, children grow up embracing moral relativism and secular ideologies, and these have become their gods. In the absence of fathers to lead, support, and nurture their families, women have compensated either by assuming masculine roles within the family, or by constructing alternative support networks for themselves and their children. This changing dynamic has brought us to a critical juncture: we are at the beginning of a fundamental shift in family life where, in the near future, if we men continue to follow the trends of the culture, fathers may be considered to be optional or unnecessary.

There is hope, but it requires hard work and sacrifice. We can adopt the words of the Apostle Paul to the young bishop Timothy to lay the foundation for getting fathers back on track: "But as for you, man of God . . . pursue righteousness, godliness, faith, love, endurance, gentleness. Fight the good fight of the faith; take hold of the eternal life, to which you were called . . ." (1 Tim 6:11–12). These virtues are the wellspring that flows from the blood of Christ on the Cross, from which we fathers must drink deeply in order to live the faith with fervor and humility. We must willingly and lovingly lay down our lives in continuous acts of service and sacrifice for our wives and children as we bear witness to the awesome power and testimony of the crucified Christ. We must embrace what is called servant leadership, with a love that is based more on a commitment of the will than on the passions or pleasures of the moment.

Mothers, who share equally in the parenting task, are the heart of love, and the love they carry within them flows from the very heart of God himself. They share that love in so many ways, especially in their tireless commitment to the family. That love must be focused and centered in a marriage covenant with her husband, who should exercise leadership in the home through his role as servant of his wife and children. No decision a father makes can be his alone: he must place the best interests of his family above everything else.

Just as Jesus called men to the priesthood to serve his Bride the Church, he also calls men through Baptism to be "priests" of the domestic church, the church of the home. In this way, a father lives out his part in the universal priesthood of the laity, which all the faithful receive at Baptism. A priest is one who offers sacrifice to God. Sacramentally ordained priests stand *in persona Christi* to offer the body and blood of Jesus at Mass. In the priesthood of the laity, which men share with women and children, fathers are called to be leaders in sacrificing themselves for their families. A father must accept the responsibility of living the Gospel by his words and actions, which can be a supreme challenge in a world filled with temptation and sin. It takes discipline and self-control to hone virtue and holiness within the family. But if they do not discipline and control themselves, fathers will not be able to serve their families as the center of order and leadership in the home.

Yet disciplining children must never be done out of anger or frustration. The goal of discipline is to *disciple* our children, to bring them into a deeper, more loving relationship with Jesus. Christ-centered discipline includes both listening with an open heart, and establishing clear and unambiguous rules concerning acceptable and unacceptable behaviors, all done with patience and understanding. A father should always show the greatest respect for his wife, serving as a model for the children on how to treat their mother, and he must be especially vigilant in shielding her from a child's rude or angry behavior. In the same spirit, decisions regarding how discipline is structured and implemented are made by father and mother together, but the father, as the spiritual head of the family, should be the primary disciplinarian. If the father is not present at the time a disciplinary measure is employed, he must back up his wife's decisions and actions, so that the children will respect her authority as well. The old saying, "Wait till your father gets home," has become a cliché, but it expresses a basic truth about a father's authority, which a mother should always feel comfortable in invoking. Both Mom and children always know that a father's authority is only a phone call away.

It is important that the type and degree of discipline be decided on before it is given to a child and that as parents you do not disagree about discipline in front of the children.

In modeling your fatherhood and authority on God the Father, you are called to ensure stability and harmony within the family. You do this by playing an active and consistent role in the lives of your children, including their education and prayer life. Men, you may feel like you are being stretched beyond your bounds (maybe like Jesus on the Cross) as you strive not only to discipline but to nurture your children. Seek, if possible, to work at a job that does not cause division within the family but rather provides for security, unity, and tranquility. That means being home for dinner as often as possible, and devoting time on weekends to family activities. By being an example of what it means to live and act as a man of God, you show your children firsthand what a personal relationship with Jesus looks like and how that relationship is lived out daily within the truth and beauty of our Catholic faith.

This all may sound too ideal, and we fathers are aware of how short we fall. I know I do. Yet I also know firsthand that it's never too late to change your ways. After years of not having a meaningful relationship with my own father, much to my surprise, he finally came to embrace the Cross. He opened himself deeply to the love, peace, and joy of discipleship in Christ, and began to live this reality every day of his life. Through Christ, we were able to repair our relationship. My father discovered what all fathers must learn: it is only when we begin to understand the gift of vulnerability and humility of the Cross that we will know what fatherhood is all about, for it is in giving ourselves away in love that we truly find ourselves in God. Seeing my own dad go through this process has helped me on my own journey as a father.

Any man can be there when a child is conceived, but it takes a real man to be a father throughout life. When our children see us living the Catholic faith with fidelity and joy, then we can be sure that our actions will be worth more than a thousand words and have confidence that our love for Christ will be written into the hearts of our sons and daughters. When we *disciple* our children, the Catholic faith will no longer become a fond memory that fades from their hearts over time. A father's living witness to covenant love and intimacy will become his enduring legacy, a precious gift for his children, and a sure sign of hope in God's endless mercy and love. I know from experience that it's never too late for a father to return to his son, or a son to his father.

7

The Best Sex You Will Ever Have

Jonathan Doyle

There is a reason you have never tried to dry your hair with a blowtorch or hammer a nail with a fish. The first would be painful and the second, while amusing, would be ineffective and equally messy. While the trend of our modern society is to believe that all things are relative and up for negotiation depending on your perspective—the "dictatorship of relativism" that Pope Benedict XVI has spoken about—the universe operates on certain laws that quietly laugh at our desires to remodel reality. The human person was made for distinct purposes and has distinct ends. We are a certain kind of being, with an identity, an essential character that is found ultimately in God, our creator.

As the *Catechism of the Catholic Church* states: "God created everything for man, but man in turn was created to serve and love God and to offer all creation back to him" (358). In other words, we come from God and are destined to return to him in love.

The ancient Greeks believed that what something *did* was a function of what it was. If so, what should human persons *do*, how should they *live* based on what they *are*? What will make them happy? What will bring them true joy? These may sound like abstract questions, but trust me, I am getting to the topic that drew you to read this chapter—how God has planned for you to have wonderful sex in your marriage. Sex, you see, is a very good thing, but it is best enjoyed in a very particular context—a context of true, stable, and permanent human love, fidelity, and mutual self-giving. We will explore why this is so, and how so many people who are searching for the "best sex ever" are going about it all wrong.

Let's return to the question about the human person, which is not just a matter for philosophy books. In fact, the wrong answers to questions about human nature throughout history have cost millions of innocent people their lives. From Auschwitz to the gulag, from ethnic cleansing to the scourge of abortion, the slaughter of millions continues in one form or another; and it can only happen when we see life as ultimately meaningless and expendable. When you believe a person is just a random collection of carbon atoms existing by chance in an uncaring universe, what's to stop one person from using another, or the stronger from oppressing the weaker, or of someone herding people into camps or killing them to recycle their organs? All this can happen when we get the facts about what a person is all wrong.

In contrast, if persons have their origin in God and are destined for eternity, each one has a higher purpose and an indelible dignity—what the Declaration of Independence calls "unalienable rights" bestowed by the Creator.

What does this have to do with marriage?

The revelation of Christ, the tenets of the Bible, and the consistent teaching of the Church make an astounding claim about who you (and your spouse) actually are. You are made in *imago Dei* or *imago Trinitatis.* You are made in the image of almighty God himself, of the eternal Trinity. Your intellect, your free will, your conscience, your immortal soul are all reflections of the one true God. From here on it gets a little more complex since we need some insight into the nature of the Trinity.

The Trinity is a perfect, always existing communion of persons—Father, Son, and Holy Spirit. There exists within the Trinity a perfect eternal exchange of pure self-giving love. Within the Trinity love is generative and love is receptive. The Father, Son, and Holy Spirit—three Persons in one God—are bonded and united in perfect love. They give love, receive love, and share love perfectly with one another and creation, especially with mankind, which is uniquely capable of receiving and returning God's love.

Now stop for a minute and consider the fact that you are made in the image of this perfect communion of love. Yes, wounded by sin but still bearing the mark of God's original gift. Each human person is called, through grace, to become more clearly an image of this love in the Trinity, through love and service of God, and love and service of neighbor. For those called to marriage, God's love is given a particular expression that generates new life not only in the spirit, but also in the flesh when the "two become one" and conceive a third person, a child.

Married couples should become more aware of the high calling of their vows and the dignity of their marital embrace in the eyes of God. As Blessed John Paul II stated in his apostolic letter on the dignity of women:

> . . . man and woman, created as a "unity of the two" in their common humanity, are called to live in a communion of love, and in this way to mirror in the world the communion of love that is in God, through which the Three Persons love each other in the intimate mystery of the one divine life. (*Mulieris Dignitatem*, III:7)

The sexual act in marriage can be seen as symbolizing, in a sense, the *total gift* of self that exists within the very core of the Trinity. This is an extraordinary elevation of the purpose and meaning of sexuality and self-giving. Although there is no way to equate the self-giving and generative love within the Trinity with the dynamics of the marital embrace, an analogy can be drawn to show just how highly God and the Church value marriage and marital sexual love. A comparison can be drawn between the Trinity as a communion of perfect love that creates new life outside itself, and the married couple as a sacramental communion in which, by God's grace, love between the spouses increases and new life for the world is generated outside itself.

This is a profound revelation of the meaning of our bodies and the meaning and significance of the sexual union in marriage. Upon hearing about this for the first time, many people find it difficult to make a link between sexual intercourse and the loving and generative nature of God. But St. Paul makes the link for us when he writes that when spouses unite as "one flesh" they are an image of Christ's self-giving love for the Church (cf. Eph 5:31–32).

By their faithful and exclusive love, including their sexual union, spouses mirror in the world the perfect love and identity of the Trinity. As Catholics, one of the best things we can do for society is to realize, value, and elevate the incredibly profound meaning of each and every act of sexual union.

By speaking the truth with our bodies, we bring truth into the world and we create communities (families) of stability and love that witness to our neighbors, work colleagues, and friends. Cardinal Angelo Scola also helps us to realize the significance of sexual intimacy when he talks about how married couples "actuate" the presence of God in the culture through their sexual union:

> In the Trinity the three persons are united in the love of a single divine Good, identical in each one. The "children of God" who live in communion actuate this dimension of the *imago Trinitatis* (cf. *Gaudium et Spes* 24) which is eminently fulfilled in the conjugal communion (cf. *Gaudium et Spes* 12).[1]

---

1. Angelo Cardinal Scola, *The Nuptial Mystery*, trans. Michelle K. Borras (Grand Rapids, MI: William B. Eerdmans Publishing Company, 2005), 29.

Unfortunately, there is a good chance you have never heard the comparison of spousal love to the love of the Trinity. It seems that the good news about married sexual union has yet to make it into the average parish. How can you deliver the good news? For a start, in your own marriage begin by realizing that every instance of sexual union mirrors something of what is taking place in the heart of the Trinity. Every moment is an opportunity to love your wife as Christ loves the Church, to place her needs above your own, to focus on her good and welfare beyond your own, and to accept her love in return.

Why would Catholic men do this? It's because our deepest and truest identity as men is to make a gift of ourselves in love. This is the truest meaning of what it is to be human. You will never be happier or more fully yourself than in the moment of self-donation, that moment where your male strength is externalized in the love and service of something beyond itself.

A big hurdle for Catholic couples on this journey to recover the joy and meaning of married sexual love is the question of contraception. Why do non-contracepting couples report higher rates of sexual satisfaction and lower rates of divorce? Again, it's a matter of identity. If we understand that we are made in the image of the Trinity, we know that love is *total* self-gift. *Nothing* is withheld. To withhold one's fertility through an act of contraception is to speak a lie with the body.

The sexual act is, in its essence, an act of total self-donation in which we hold nothing back from our spouse. To contracept is to speak only part of the truth to my spouse. It is to say, "I withhold from you my fertility, this deep aspect of who I am, this aspect of the truth of my body." The fact that both spouses agree to contracept does not make it less of a lie; it simply means both withhold the truth of their fertility from each other.

This does not mean that a family has to have a tribe of children. It does mean that we can use the techniques of Natural Family Planning that help both husband and wife develop a certain awe and reverence for the natural cycles of fertility. For most men, NFP will be challenging with its periods of abstinence, but it is also an opportunity to unite these challenges with the redemptive work of Christ and to make use of the helps of the Church, including the Eucharist, to grow in virtue and selfless love. Remember that this is also a challenge for your wife. Your closeness in living the faith as a couple will bring strength and joy even amid the challenges of life.

The Catholic vision of sex, marriage, and love is a story about God and about you as a Catholic man, and about you and your bride as a couple. It's about who God is, and about both of you, made in his image. Like the example of the blowtorch hairdryer and the fish hammer with which I began, if we use our bodies in ways that contradict their nature it just doesn't work. Our bodies are made for communion, for relationship, here on earth and ultimately in heaven. Think for a moment about how much pain and sadness exist in the world due to the lack of understanding of this simple truth.

This message of selfless love runs against the mindset of our time that wants pleasure without commitment and sex without children. But a Catholic man must get his message from God. It is a question of whether or not you will partner with God through grace and sacrament to be the man you are called to be.

Let me close with a quote that Karen, my wife, often shares with men when she speaks at conferences: "You can tell the quality of a man by the smile on his wife's face."

8

Theology of the Body for Fathers

DAMON C. OWENS

What does fatherhood mean? Is there any deeper meaning beyond "making babies"? Does a deeper meaning even matter? There is indeed a profound meaning of fatherhood that must be reclaimed not only for our happiness today, but also for our eternal happiness.

Rightly understood, fatherhood is the vocation of every man, because first and foremost it is a *spiritual* engendering that may—or may not—include begetting biological children. In whatever way we express it, we are created for life-giving love, which may include adopting a child, mentoring a child, teaching a child, or giving "new life" to others through our exercise of faith, hope, and charity. If we have biological children, of course, our fatherhood does not end with procreation. We need to be present and engaged with our children throughout life in ways appropriate to their age.

In this light, fatherhood is a state of personal maturity wherein we desire, master, and direct our power to engender life outside of ourselves. It is a sexual power because it is expressed through our male body, and a divine power because it is a participation in God's own creative power. It is far broader and deeper than we realize because it originates in God the Father, who from the beginning has inscribed this life-giving aspiration into our being—body and soul—as part of the mystery of being made in his "image and likeness." A human father is a good father to the extent that he reflects God the Father in his own life and vocation. This goal is not a distant, spiritualistic abstraction. God's love is made knowable to us in and through our concrete human experiences, most particularly through human experiences of love.

The challenge is before us men. Now more than ever, the world, the Church, our community, and our family need our fatherhood. We need, in turn, a means truly to see our vocation to fatherhood even in the midst of our own sin and brokenness. Fortunately, there is something we know well that will reveal this mystery of fatherhood if we look at it in a new way: the human body itself.

The first thing we must understand is that our body and soul belong together. The belief that the body is somehow evil and the spirit pure is all too common, but this view is not Catholic teaching. Rather, the Church teaches that our body gives expression to our soul, and the two will be united after death for eternity. That is how much God esteems our flesh. And this fact is the foundation of Blessed John Paul II's great work *Man and Woman He Created Them: A Theology of the Body*, often referred to simply as Theology of the Body or TOB.

> The body, in fact, and only the body, is capable of making visible what is invisible: the spiritual and divine. It has been created to transfer into the visible reality of the world the mystery hidden from eternity in God, and thus to be a sign of it. (TOB 19:4)

Delivered in a series of talks from September 1979 to November 1984, TOB is an invitation to discover the prophetic meaning of our bodies as an enduring revelation of our call to life-giving love. The body is an effective sign—a kind of sacrament—that serves as a witness to human love in God's divine plan. This call or vocation to love, to make a gift of self, flows from *"reading the 'language of the body' in the truth"* (TOB 118:6). In concrete ways, the body, as male and female, speaks the language of communion: the two are made for one another.

Masculinity and femininity expressed through the body make sense only in light of the other. Each can be seen as directing us away from solitude or selfishness and toward a common union, or communion. What John Paul II called the "spousal meaning of the body" recalls our *origin* "in the image and likeness of God," moves us into *history* with the sacramentality of marriage, and points us toward our heavenly *destiny* in the redemption of the body.

TOB offers an integral or whole vision of our humanity that not only rejects a false conflict between body and soul, but invites us to recognize (literally re-*know*) the great mysteries of the Trinity, Christ and the Church, sexuality, marriage, and heaven *through* the body. Sex—male and female—makes visible the call we all have to make a "sincere gift of self."

Reflecting on man's origin, history, and eternal destiny as a body-person is a worthy point from which to explore the deep mystery of fatherhood.

In the beginning, prior to sin entering the world, our first parents discovered a "spousal" meaning of their bodies created as male and female (Gen 2:23–25). Their bodies expressed externally the interior call to be a gift—to love as God loves in life-giving communion. Sexual difference and complementarity (and, in fact, sexual desire) are a sign and a calling that orients our existence toward divinity. Before sin, Adam and Eve's true freedom allowed them to experience sexual attraction as nothing other than the desire to make a sincere gift of themselves to the other and to receive the other's sincere gift. This makes all the more sense in light of the revelation of God as a Trinitarian *communion*, in which there is one God in three divine yet distinct Persons. Our spousal unity-in-distinction is a revelation of the divine unity-in-distinction.

But because we cannot give what we do not possess, self-gift requires self-possession or self-mastery. Further, since we cannot master what we do not know, self-mastery requires self-knowledge.

> Being in the image of God the human individual possesses the dignity of a person, who is not just something, but

someone. He is capable of self-knowledge, of self-possession and of freely giving himself and entering into communion with other persons. (*Catechism of the Catholic Church*, 357)

The deeper the knowing, the stronger the call to self-mastery. And the stronger the self-mastery, the more sincere the self-gift. This dynamism of love actually forms us. It makes us more fully human. Moreover, being made in God's own image, the more human we become, the closer we come to divinity. We become what we love. When we love like God, we share in his divinity!

While the entry of sin into the world has wounded our nature—so that selfishness often replaces self-gift—we can still reread the language of our bodies in truth to discover a shadow of that good and noble beginning. Yet there is a battle raging in our hearts between the longing for communion (good) and the tendency to use others for our own pleasure (evil). Christ points to this sinful desire in the Sermon on the Mount: "You have heard that it was said, 'You shall not commit adultery.' But I say to you that everyone who looks at a woman with lust has already committed adultery with her in his heart" (Mt 5:27–28).

His warning must not be mistaken as a stifling of passion, sexual desire, or even eros. Rather, it is a call to restore these good things to serve the good of the other through our gift of self. Eros (passionate love) must be purified by agape (self-gift), just as agape must be animated by eros. One without the other makes a caricature of life and our love—particularly in marriage.

Christ implores us to "lift up our hearts" so that he can take our hearts of stone and return to us hearts of flesh full of God's own desires! The inclination to sin will be with us until the redemption of our bodies. Yet if we allow him, God can heal us from the dominance of the desire to sin, and purify our hearts, so that we see others as persons to love and not to use, and actually begin to see God in and through others. "Blessed are the pure in heart, for they will see God" (Mt 5:8).

Men, we are called to a great mission. Moving from boyhood to manhood to fatherhood to sainthood is the work of a lifetime, and it requires God's love. To love according to Christ's Great Commandment is to engender new life in others. We can begin this love today.

The small, ordinary events and encounters of our day are occasions for us to "become holy or die trying." As fathers at service to our families, we are called to "die daily" in the small things: go to bed and get up on time each day; anticipate the needs of others; listen and hold our tongue; yield in matters of personal preference; praise, encourage, affirm; speak the truth; keep high expectations and be quick to forgive; pray for grace for ourselves and for others.

However, on some level we are hurt, broken, angry, scared, or held back by shame. Our own sins have bound us, and the sins of others have crippled us. Yet love is always possible in the present moment. This is the central message of Theology of the Body for fathers—our love can make new children, and it can also renew the hearts of the children we have. As fathers, we need to live that love each day.

9

Millennials, Morality, and New Evangelization

Jason Godin

Recent studies on young people would appear to offer little hope for the future of fatherhood and the family in America. Statistics on cohabitation, single motherhood, divorce, and same-sex "marriage" indicate problems that could become worse as the Millennial Generation (those born after 1980) grows to adulthood. Yet there are many bright spots on the horizon when we recall that the millennial group includes the "John Paul II Generation"—those who grew up during that great papacy (1978–2005) and have embraced the call to a New Evangelization that continued under Pope Benedict XVI.

As a thirty-two-year-old college professor, and husband and father of two young children, I think that young Catholics can be the leaven for renewal in the present age. It will take a lot of hard work and a courageous and confident witness based on the *Catechism of the Catholic Church* and John Paul's Theology of the Body, which has the power to reach young people with a message about the harms inflicted on our hearts and health by this secular, sex-saturated society. We should look at our witness not as a crusade, but rather as a service of love, to bring the balm of healing to those who don't know why they are hurting. This is the essence of the New Evangelization.

It won't be easy. Studies suggest that the Millennial Generation is connected technologically, divided physically, and adrift morally. Starting in 2006, the Pew Research Center has conducted surveys on social attitudes among eighteen to twenty-nine-year-olds as part of a report called "Millennials: A Portrait of Generation Next." In February 2010, an initial report was released, stating that the Millennial Generation was the first "always connected" generation in history, with 75 percent in that group having a profile on a social network site. The same report added that millennials value parenthood far more than marriage; they distinguish "one of the most important things" in life as "being a good parent" over "having a successful marriage" by a ratio of 52 percent to 30 percent.

Millennials also are less likely than previous generations to have grown up in intact families.[1]

Additional results published in March 2011 produced deeper insights into how millennials view marriage and parenting. On marriage as an institution, 44 percent thought it was "becoming obsolete" and 46 percent found the "growing variety in family arrangements" to be a "good thing." When asked about the reasons for marriage, 49 percent answered "having children" as "very important," significantly behind "love" (88 percent), "making a lifelong commitment" (76 percent), and "companionship" (71 percent). The report also revealed that 51 percent of births among the Millennial Generation were to unmarried couples, yet 53 percent believed that a child needed both a father and mother to grow up happily.[2]

Perhaps some of the apparent contradictions in the surveys can be explained by the fact that so many millennials have lived through the divorce of their parents, an experience that could make them skeptical about marriage but certain that children need a mother and father at home. Indeed, an overwhelming amount of data supports the vital importance of an

---

1. Paul Taylor and Scott Keeter, eds., "Millennials: A Portrait of Generation Next," Pew Research Center (February 2010), Preface, pp. 1–2, 53. http://www.pewsocial trends.org/files/2010/10/millennials-confident-connected-open-to-change.pdf.

2. Paul Taylor et al., "For Millennials, Parenthood Trumps Marriage," Pew Research Center (March 9, 2011), pp. 3, 4, 6, 12. http://www.pewsocialtrends.org/files/2011/03/millennials-marriage.pdf.

intact family. Summarizing the findings of multiple studies by government agencies and sociologists, the National Fatherhood Initiative reports that children living without their biological father at home are *five times* more likely to live in poverty and are at greater risk for dangers such as substance abuse. A child living in a single-parent home is twice as likely to suffer physical, emotional, or educational neglect, and children without fathers at home are also twice as likely to either repeat a grade or drop out of school.[3]

With nonmarital births today accounting for a bit over half of all Millennial Generation babies, and with only a slight majority of millennials thinking that it takes two parents to raise a child, the trend looks bleak for fatherhood. Yet we must not become discouraged, because these present trends are not inevitable. It took about fifty years for our culture to move from the nuclear family norm to its present state, and it may take that long to move it back. But move it we must, for the sake of our own children and grandchildren. Fortunately, we have a road map for action.

Catholic men of all ages have received a summons to witness to their faith in the New Evangelization called for by our recent popes. In February 1994 John Paul II issued a *Letter to Families* that explored fatherhood, motherhood, and the family together as "*the centre and the heart of the civilization of love.*"[4] Three years later, the pope approved the final edition

---

3. National Fatherhood Initiative, "The Facts on Father Absence." http://www.fatherhood.org/page.aspx?pid=403.

4. John Paul II, *Letter to Families* (Vatican City: Libreria Editrice Vaticana, 1994), 13.

of the *Catechism*, which he called a "genuine, systematic presentation of the faith and of Catholic doctrine," and he urged all the faithful to present, "with renewed fervor, each and every part of the Christian message to the people of our time."[5] In 2005 Benedict XVI echoed his predecessor, warning that "no people can ignore the precious good of the family, founded on marriage," if "they are to give a truly human face to society."[6]

The *Catechism* defines matrimony as an "intimate communion of life and love" both beneficial and bountiful because it is "ordered to the good of the couple" as well as "to the generation and education of children." Marriage is a sacrament that provides husband and wife "grace to love each other" with "the love with which Christ has loved his Church." Together spouses experience unique graces because the holy union "perfects the human love of spouses, strengthens their indissoluble unity, and sanctifies them on the way to eternal life."[7]

Drawing from this rich teaching on human love and responsibility, and responding to the Church's call, laypeople also are taking a leadership role in the New Evangelization. In his 2008 bestselling book *A Civilization of Love*, Carl Anderson, head of the 1.8-million member Knights of Columbus, analyzed the teachings of John Paul II and Benedict XVI to

---

5. John Paul II, Apostolic Letter *Laetamur Magnopere*, Aug. 15, 1997.

6. Benedict XVI, "Letter to Participants in the Fifth World Meeting of Families," May 17, 2005.

7. *Catechism of the Catholic Church*, 1, 660–61.

identify the purpose, place, and potential of the family in the modern world. Quoting John Paul's insight that the "current of the civilization of love"[8] passes through the family, Anderson writes that the family is "the first and greatest bulwark" against "encroachment of lifelessness and materialism of contemporary culture." It serves as a "setting in which new life is brought into the world and nurtured to the point where it can survive independently," as well as the primary "vehicle for transmitting to the rising generation the values that will shape it and guide it into the future." Anderson concluded that the family holds "the ultimate fate of the human race" and "the ultimate fate of the family lies in the integrity of the intimate life of husband and wife."[9]

Indeed, men who embrace the New Evangelization celebrate marriage as a holy gift shared with their wives, recognize sex as the expression of love exclusive to that union, and share the responsibility for the children that may come of their loving embrace.

The growth of Catholic men's conferences is another sign that laypeople are taking up the call of the New Evangelization and that fathers are ready to live their faith in a way that can change the culture. At these gatherings, which have sprung up in dioceses across the United States, inspirational speakers challenge men to step up in their families and in the public

---

8. John Paul II, *Letter to Families* (Vatican City: Libreria Editrice Vaticana, 1994), 15.

9. Carl Anderson, *A Civilization of Love: What Every Catholic Can Do to Transform the World* (New York: HarperCollins, 2008), p. 81.

square, to take leadership in passing on the faith and protecting their families from the harmful influences of our culture. They are called to become "pure warriors," who enter battles like knights of old, through hours of prayer and the sacrament of Confession.

These are wonderful ideals, worthy of a man's life and total devotion. Yet when I view the Millennial Generation, I see mixed signs. I see that so few consider same-sex "marriage" as undermining the very nature of marriage and the family. Rather, a vague sense of "diversity" seems to trump the definite value of a husband and wife raising their children—a value most millennials consider important.

Yet I do see a sign of hope in the strong and increasing pro-life sentiment of young people. Growing up under the regime of *Roe vs. Wade*, they clearly have a problem with unrestricted abortion on demand. In a 2010 Marist College Institute for Public Opinion/Knights of Columbus poll, a full 58 percent of millennials said that abortion was morally wrong.[10] Our challenge is to help millennials build on that pro-life majority and show them how the underlying truth about the dignity of the human person extends to other issues such as marriage, family, and childbearing.

The moment is now. I see in my college classroom every day that "Generation Next" is coming of age. Like young people of every era, they are idealistic, energetic, and

---

10. "American Millennials: Generations Apart," Marist College Institute for Public Opinion/Knights of Columbus, Feb. 11, 2010, http://www.kofc.org/un/en/resources/communications/documents/poll_mil_religion.pdf.

seeking an identity. They are searching for meaning and to make a difference. We must reach them with the voice of the John Paul II Generation which began with the pope's words, "Be not afraid!" We must open to them the riches of the Theology of the Body, which explains the basis of the human desire for "love," "making a lifelong commitment," and "companionship" that the Pew surveys show they value so highly. Well-versed in the truths of our faith, fathers in the New Evangelization should be unafraid and full of hope for the next generation. We must answer young people's questions and respond to their natural quest for happiness with a "yes" that will keep them listening to the voice of the Church. If we don't hold out this hope in Christ, the voice of the world may overtake them, and the next generation will tune us out.

10

Superdad:
More Than an Action Figure

Bill Donaghy

I'm convinced that every dad might be a superhero in the making, destined for greatness. Sure, we might appear as mild-mannered insurance salesmen, construction workers, or lawn care and outdoor grill specialists, but underneath that seemingly mundane surface, there's more. By virtue of the grace of sacramental marriage, dads can be faster than a speeding stroller, more powerful than a poopy diaper, and able to leap tall bushes in a single bound when the health and safety of the family is at stake. We are called, in the words of Blessed John Paul II, to embrace our *natural greatness*.

So why do there appear to be so few Superdads in the workplace, the malls, the town greens, and the parish halls of daily life? Many speak of a crisis in fatherhood and a collapse of the family structure in general. My hypothesis is simple— there's a lot of kryptonite out there. According to studies, more than 30 million children in the United States do not have a father living with them. Ninety percent of all homeless and runaway children do not have their father in their lives. Seventy percent of juveniles in state institutions and 85 percent of all youths in prisons grew up in a fatherless home. Father absence is a scourge across our nation, and across generations.

Clearly, there are seductive forces that seek to steal away a father's heart from his greatest mission: the health and safety of his wife and children. These forces that sap dads of their powers aren't as obvious as the evil villains we see in the movies, all cloaked in shadow, but they are strong nonetheless. It might be the lure of money and financial security that leads Dad to become a workaholic. It could be his basic need for rest and relaxation that morphs into laziness when the family calls down to the "man cave" for help. Perhaps the vocation to self-giving, sacrificial love has been diverted now to personal pleasure, sought out in pornography or the accumulation of possessions. To be a Superdad one must have a vigilant heart to resist distraction; a little X-ray vision to see through the shallowness of these temptations would help as well.

But here is the good news. A father's superpowers are still there even when misused, abandoned, or simply not fully developed. They glow steady and strong in the secret chambers of a man's heart, often waiting to be unlocked by the hands of a child. When that new life comes, it can draw him out of himself. New and fragile human life can be that clarion call to a guy once again to "man up" and realize that his life is no longer his own. It must be a complete self-gift for others. We've been called to greatness, to be a light to the family, to love and protect in good times and in bad. This mission began in the great leap of faith we made into marriage, and grows deeper still as children come from that marital embrace.

Do we men allow ourselves to return to that original fountain of grace for renewal, our sacramental marriage? It is the heart of our vocation, and this spousal covenant really does have the power to transform us. Remember when you said, "I do"? It was not just for that one moment. What you were really saying was, "I always will." But sometimes we need to be reminded of that commitment. As Pope Benedict XVI has written, "Love is the very process of passing over, of transformation, of stepping outside the limitations of fallen humanity—in which we are all separated from one another . . . into an infinite otherness."[1] Sounds good to me!

When Superman needed a refresher on who he was and what he was called to do, he returned to his Fortress of Solitude. Fathers need to return to a special place as well, to discern and discover their unique call. Let's call it the Fortress of

---

1. Benedict XVI, *Jesus of Nazareth, Part Two: Holy Week from the Entrance into Jerusalem to the Resurrection* (San Francisco: Ignatius Press, 2011), 54–55.

Communion—our marriage! It's that place of sacramental grace where the two became one flesh. Marriage is that holy ground where the seed of our superpowers was first planted.

These powers (otherwise known as *virtues*) often build slowly, as in the old TV series *Greatest American Hero*. The character Ralph Hinkley, a mild-mannered high school teacher, was given a "super suit" but lost the "instruction manual." Each week he had to discover, as all new dads do, how it all works. For Hinkley, there was much trial and error, yet he became the *Greatest American Hero* by allowing the "grace" of the super suit to build on his willing-though-weak human nature. That's actually good Catholic theology. God's grace is not magic; it builds on human nature, and on the skills and strength we develop. God is always willing to give—like that super suit was always ready to perform—but we men must grow in virtue in order to use that grace to its fullest. How do we do this?

For a Catholic dad, the instruction manual is revealed in Sacred Scripture, and the "super suit" is the grace first given at our Baptism. Our skills are strengthened with every sacramental encounter since that day, including Mass, Confession, Holy Eucharist, and our Marriage. So long as we dads stick close to those healing rays that strengthen us, the kryptonite of selfishness can't overcome our hearts. Like Superman gaining strength from the light of the sun, our strength flows from the Son of God. I've discovered this personally. I need the ritual of prayer, the light of Christ's rays beaming from the Eucharist, to make me a better husband and father.

Every superhero needs a mentor. Just as Jesus mentors me, so I must pass on what I receive to my children—an apprenticeship that is handed on generation to generation. Our way to God the Father is always shown to us first through our earthly fathers. I still have pictures in my mind's eye of my dad. He wasn't always perfect. Like the *Greatest American Hero*, he could be clumsy at times, as I am sometimes today. But through his cooperation with grace, he grew stronger. I can still see him in the wee hours of the night kneeling before the little statue of the Blessed Mother in the living room, clutching his rosary. He made visits to the Blessed Sacrament, he fasted, and he kept his vows after a painful divorce.

I continue to learn from my father's devotion to prayer that an inseparable connection must be made between my role as father and my love for my heavenly Father. As St. Paul wrote to the Ephesians, "For this reason I bow my knees before the Father, from whom every family in heaven and on earth takes its name" (Eph 3:14–15). As a relatively new dad myself (our Boy Wonder is 3 years old, and Super Girl is 1), I can see they already watch my moves. My son has nearly perfected the genuflection, though his aim is slightly off, and his sign of the cross is really coming together. For my daughter, too, my faith must be ever present, and my gaze upon her full of love and affirmation so that she may one day look upon herself as that gift for others that every person is called to be.

All of this is best accomplished hand in hand with my wife. Together in Christ, we can be an unstoppable force. We can build that fortress of Communion to give our children a firm grounding and a sure identity in Christ. Showing them how to maintain this identity in a world of distractions is our greatest mission. It is the mission of the family to whom is entrusted—as John Paul II wrote in his *Letter to Families*—"the task of striving, first and foremost, *to unleash the forces of good.*" [2]

Let the adventure begin!

---

2. Blessed John Paul II, *Letter to Families*, 23.

11

You *Can* Keep
Your Kids Catholic

PATRICK MADRID

There are very few things a father can give his children that will last forever—the latest digital gadget, a trust fund, and even a college education are good only for this lifetime. But there are some eternal gifts that a dad should be careful to pass on. They include love and its greatest expression in the Holy Eucharist. That is, the Catholic faith.

If we cherish this faith as we should, we want to see our children embrace it as well. Yet there are so many examples of kids leaving the Catholic Church for some other Christian denomination or even abandoning religion altogether. Their parents can feel like failures, and tense and even hostile attitudes can build up.

In this chapter, I will outline some practices that have worked in the Madrid household so that all eleven of our children remain practicing Catholics. I hope that you, as a father, can benefit from my experience.

First, Dad, never underestimate your influence or let your wife "take care of the religion" alone. Research indicates that if a father practices his faith and takes his children to Mass, the odds are great that they will stay in the Church. A dad who skips Mass or prefers Sunday football will devastate the faith of his children. So step up and join your wife in handing on the faith.

Indeed, we cannot underestimate the importance of parental influence. There is a great and powerful effect when Mom and Dad themselves live out as best they can their own love for God, in visible but not ostentatious ways, through prayer, piety, and sacramental life.

As Scripture says, "Train children in the right way, and when old, they will not stray" (Prov 22:6). Children need firm guidance and good example from their youngest years so they will grow upright in their knowledge and love of God. The good example from Mom and Dad, as well as clear and purposeful handing on of the truths of the faith, are essential.

You don't need a theology degree for this task, but you do need to make a diligent effort to impart a basic knowledge of the Catholic faith and set an example for your children on how to really live out that faith. You wouldn't expect your children to take you seriously if all you had was grade school knowledge of money or budgeting. In the same way, if you never try to learn and grow in your own knowledge of and love for the Catholic faith, they could easily conclude that the faith is not very important to you. As they grow, they may go elsewhere with their questions about God and life.

The first step you need to take is to let your children know that the Catholic faith is more than an hour a week on Sunday. Weekly Mass should be the highlight and absolute obligation of the week, but it doesn't end there. A Catholic home is a sort of "domestic church," as Blessed John Paul II and others have noted. This does not mean Gregorian chant and incense at the dinner table. But it does mean that faith must inform the daily routine and decisions in the home. Children must see Mom and Dad as truly prayerful, again not in a showy way, but in a way where they know—because they can see—that their parents look to God trustingly and are not too proud to ask for help from above.

I strongly encourage praying the family Rosary. If you, the father of the family, trustingly invoke the powerful intercession of the Blessed Virgin Mary each day on behalf of your family, you can rest assured that, no matter how bumpy the road of life may become, she will be there helping you. It may be a challenge at times to gather the whole family together, but the spiritual benefits of praying the Rosary are enormous, especially if each child is allowed to recite a part of this beautiful prayer. Other essentials are prayer before and after meals (every meal), and night prayers such as the Act of Contrition and the Prayer to St. Michael the Archangel.

In our home, when our kids get to be about twelve, my wife and I give them their own personal Bible with a loving inscription from us inside the cover. And we strongly encourage them to read Scripture often, starting with the Gospels. We have two goals in mind. First, our children learn that the Bible is not a "Protestant thing" and should be cherished by all Catholics. Also, they learn to discover the biblical basis for a wide range of Catholic teachings and practices.

Beyond the externals of prayer and piety in the home, children need to see that Mom and Dad are imbued with the results of prayer—that they actually live out the gifts of faith, hope, and charity. Having kids in the home is a constant source for examination of conscience. A father does well to tell his kids not to gossip, but does he talk about the neighbors uncharitably? After telling his children not to talk back or show disrespect, does he then turn and shout at his wife? This sends the message that religion is for hypocrites.

Of course, no father is perfect, and our children will understand this too, but I believe that they must see men who love God and are doing their very best, by God's grace, to live the faith. In this respect, let your children see you frequent the sacrament of Confession because you too fall short and need God's pardon.

Setting a good example at home is the first step, but what happens when the kids go into the world? Entering college is one of the most crucial crossroads for young Catholics, and fathers must be vigilant in helping them through this rite of passage. Far too many kids lose their faith on campus, even at so-called Catholic colleges.

Kids can be swayed by an atheist professor, or drawn out of the Church by aggressive evangelicals who use the Bible to challenge Catholic beliefs. Or, if they don't abandon the faith for some substitute ideology (atheism, skepticism, secularism), it sometimes happens that they succumb to what might be called in biblical terms "the world, the flesh, and the devil," known today as "sex, drugs, and rock 'n' roll." There are lots of moral and spiritual dangers awaiting your children in college. Thus, I believe very much in the practice of "inoculation," to prepare your kids now for what they will face later.

I tell my kids what atheists believe and what skepticism and relativism are, and I give them the answers to these and similar challenges. I also tell them about the errors of Protestants and how to answer their challenges right from the Bible. Education in sexual purity should be ongoing, but you must clearly express your expectation that they remain chaste and healthy. Your kids may not immediately understand the importance of everything you tell them. But when they do come against these challenges (and they will), they will remember what you said and this will reinforce in their minds the fact that their dad is someone who knows about the world and how to deal with it. They will be even more confident in coming to you about other important matters, such as sex, marriage, career, and money. What dad wouldn't want that!

But you've got to earn that status. Just as your favorite sports star has to work to reach the top of his game, so you as a father have to expend some effort to keep your kids Catholic. Get educated yourself. Don't be afraid to crack the binding of that family Bible, or open the *Catechism of the Catholic Church*, or go online to reputable Catholic websites. We live in an information age, and there is a vast amount of good Catholic resources right at your fingertips. God has put you on this earth at this time, and given you these children, and he expects you to make good use of these resources to help your children become strong in the faith.

Fatherhood is a great joy and a great privilege, but we must never forget that it is also an awesome responsibility given to us by God the Father. What greater joy could you possibly have than to pass on the riches of the Catholic faith as a permanent, priceless inheritance to your children? If they have their Catholic faith and a true love for God, they have everything. Pray that they will eventually rejoice with you in heaven, thanking God and thanking you for the fatherly gifts that you bestowed on them. That is your mission as a father.

12

Repairing a Broken Marriage

Peter C. Kleponis

We all know someone who is divorced, and maybe we have considered the possibility ourselves. It seems that our society has accepted the belief that if people aren't happy in marriage, it's okay to call it quits. Yet research shows that people who decide to stick it out and work through their problems can be happier in the long run than those who opt for divorce. So what can a couple do to save their marriage when it seems like it's broken beyond repair?

At that point, it may be time to call a professional marriage counselor who understands and respects Catholic teachings, can assess the relationship, and can offer a plan for healing and reconciliation. Going this route requires great humility and courage for a couple; however, the result can be a recovered and fulfilling marriage. Isn't that what we all wanted when we said, "I do"?

When examining their relationship with a therapist, both the husband and wife need to willingly take responsibility for the problems in the marriage. They must be willing to point a finger at themselves, and not just at the other. Even if only 10 percent of the problems are caused by one spouse, that partner must be willing to make the necessary changes for healing and reconciliation.

Each spouse also needs to be able to see what he or she brought into the marriage from the families-of-origin that could be having a negative impact on the relationship. Face it, we all have baggage! Most often, the problems within a marriage didn't start the minute the couple tied the knot. When the issues both people bring into the marriage are combined, the problems may seem insurmountable and reconciliation hopeless. This can be seen in the case of a couple we'll call Bob and Joan, who are typical of the many couples I have worked with over years of professional practice.

Bob and Joan had been married for ten years, and when they came for counseling, neither seemed too hopeful or interested in repairing their marriage. Years of anger and frustration left them feeling bitter and resentful toward each other. Fortunately, they were willing to look at their relationship and try to figure out what went wrong, at least for the sake of their children.

When asked what the main problem in the marriage was, Joan replied that it was Bob's excessive anger. Every night he would come home from work in a bad mood and take his frustrations out on Joan and the kids. It didn't matter what had angered Bob, he always took it out on his family. Weekends were just as bad. Everyone knew to "stay out of Dad's way." After ten years, Joan was ready to call it quits.

Bob had a very different view. He said Joan's emotional distance was the problem. It was very difficult for him to get close to Joan. She had little interest in sex and seemed to avoid him, like an "ice queen." Bob was extremely lonely in the marriage and also ready to call it quits.

In therapy, Joan and Bob were asked to talk about their families-of-origin. This provided much insight into their individual behaviors and how they reacted to each other.

Joan grew up in a household with a father who was an angry alcoholic and a mother who was weak and passive. The worst time of day was when her father came home from work. Joan never knew if he would be drunk or what kind of mood he would be in. Unfortunately, her mother was unable to protect the children from their father's anger, so Joan learned to avoid him as much as possible.

As an adult, Joan made a vow to herself not to marry an alcoholic. Bob was not a drinker, but he did have a temper like her father's. Because of this, she reacted to Bob in the same way she reacted to her father, by withdrawing and isolating herself. She was reliving the family dynamic she had hoped to avoid.

For his part, Bob had very cold and distant parents. His mother struggled with depression and was not nurturing and affectionate. His father was a traveling salesman and spent much of his time on the road. Growing up with such emotional deprivation resulted in a deep sadness in Bob. He craved love and attention. The frustration of not having basic emotional needs met left Bob angry.

As an adult, Bob looked for a wife who would be nurturing and affectionate, and thought he had found her in Joan. However, she was not able to meet this need. Thus, soon after they were married, Bob's anger emerged. It was especially apparent when he felt he was not getting enough attention from Joan.

Talking about their families-of-origin and their associated wounds was a real eye-opener for Bob and Joan. They had never discussed their childhoods with each other. They were finally able to understand their behaviors and how they were each contributing to marital discord. With a better understanding of their situation, each was willing to make the necessary changes to improve their relationship.

Bob and Joan's first assignment was to work on forgiving each other. Forgiveness is a process that can take some time. Understanding each other's wounds made it easier. Asking God to help them to forgive was extremely helpful in the process. In time, they were able to let go of their anger toward each other and truly forgive.

Next, they each had to work on changing their reactions toward each other. For Bob, this meant controlling his temper. In therapy, he learned to forgive the people who hurt him in the past. This prevented him from misdirecting anger toward Joan. Whenever he noticed Joan withdrawing, he knew it was a reaction to his anger. At that point, he would apologize and ask Joan for forgiveness. Seeing Bob's sincerity helped Joan forgive and feel safe with Bob.

For Joan, changing her behavior meant first understanding that Bob was not her father and she did not have to fear him. Whenever Bob did get angry, she would remind him that she should not be the recipient of his misdirected anger. Joan also worked on forgiving Bob daily for the times he hurt her. All of this helped Joan to grow in confidence, which resulted in her not needing to withdraw from Bob so often.

Their Catholic faith played a large role in healing their marriage—especially in forgiving each other. They would invite God into their therapy sessions and ask for his guidance. They also attended Mass together, prayed at home, and received the sacrament of Confession weekly. The forgiveness they received from God enabled them to forgive one another. Deep down, they knew that God wanted to bless their marriage.

In addition, both had to grieve the absence of the healthy childhoods they never had. Although addressing old wounds was painful, it opened them up to receive God's healing. They began to see God as their loving, protective Father and the Blessed Mother as their affectionate, nurturing mother. This helped to heal their deep mother and father wounds.

After several months, Bob and Joan revealed that they were once again deeply in love with each other and enjoyed their marriage. They still are in need of healing; however, they are working on this together. Their children are also much happier because they see their parents content and reconciled in their marriage.

The example of Bob and Joan shows how important it is to understand that we all enter into marriage with deep wounds that can have a negative impact on our relationship. Issues from childhood such as anger, addictions, abuse, depression, selfishness, and emotional deprivation can leave a person deeply wounded. We need to be willing to look at our lives, identify our wounds, and work on healing them. We also need to be willing to forgive, seek forgiveness, and make whatever changes are necessary to heal the relationship. Finally, we need to invite God into the process. He is the ultimate healer of hearts. Without him, I don't believe that true healing in a marriage can occur.

Key points for healing a marriage

- Don't be afraid to seek professional help.
- Admit the problems you have caused in the relationship.
- Realize that many marital problems are caused by emotional wounds brought into the marriage.
- Understand your spouse's past hurts, and your own, and how they affect the marriage.
- Work on forgiving each other.
- Be willing to change your behavior to foster healing and reconciliation.

❖ Bring God and the Blessed Mother into the healing process.

❖ Don't give up! God wants to heal you, your spouse, and your marriage.

Breaking the Chains of Porn

MARK HOUCK

Writing about the pervasiveness of pornography in our culture and its corrosive effects on men and marriage today is a dubious honor. As someone blessed to have been set free from my own sixteen-year addiction to porn, I regret that my credentials for this chapter come largely from personal experience. Yet, as there was hope for me, there is hope for others who may be trapped in the snares of pornography. God is more powerful than porn, and with his help we can be too!

Most men think, like I once did, that one glance at a pornographic image is harmless. At some warped level, we even convince ourselves that we deserve this little sneak peek—after all, we're guys with raging hormones and these willing women are just a mouse click or turn of the page away. But one look is all it takes to prime a man for a potential porn addiction. It may sound old-fashioned to say this, but I found it to be true in my case and in the cases of so many men I have met in my ministry against porn: the Father of Lies—the devil—is lurking behind those seemingly harmless images. He knows that many men who are brave, strong, and virtuous in every other aspect of their lives can be snared by the temptations of the flesh. Even though I am fairly tall and physically strong, I was weak enough to fall into one of the oldest temptations known to men. Yet with God's grace, I regained my strength.

It is no secret that men are prone to visual stimulation. Science has shown that every time a man looks at a pornographic image, a chemical reaction triggers the release of dopamine to his brain, which produces pleasurable sensations. This process reinforces the pornographic stimulation and sets a man up for an addictive cycle that is hard to break. I suspect that God created men in this way so we would notice women, literally keep them (chemically mapped) in mind, begin a relationship, and ultimately "be fruitful and multiply" (Gen 1:28). But when the women are only images, there is no relationship to be made, and no children to be created. A man can actually come to prefer the images to a real woman or even his wife because he can get a "dopamine rush" at any time by himself, without having to build and maintain a relationship. In a short time, a man can become self-centered, secretive, and hooked.

This response to a woman is far from what Adam exclaimed when he first saw Eve: "This at last is bone of my bones and flesh of my flesh" (Gen 2:23). Adam, who was without sin at the time, did not see Eve merely as an object for pleasure; rather, he recognized her as a person with the same nature and dignity as his own, who was taken out of man.

Viewers of porn have a much different response. They may experience great physical pleasure, but there is always a shadow of sorrow, grief, and apprehension toward what they view because the lovely image of the female body is being perverted and presented in an unholy manner. Most men searching for porn would not acknowledge this fact. Yet I suspect that the first time a young man sees a pornographic image, his intense curiosity over something found is mixed with sadness over innocence lost—it was for me!

Every porn addict, whether he admits it or not, knows deep in the recesses of his soul that what he is doing is wrong. He knows in his heart that what he sees is reserved for spousal love alone. Despite efforts to suppress conscience and deny that an impure moment is even happening, those who seek these images have great reason to grieve and be alarmed at this obvious violation of the dignity of the human person and the affront to the goodness of womanhood.

Yet millions of Christian men all over the world are falling for these one-glance cheap tricks of the devil. And when one look leads to another, the Evil One knows he has snared another victim in his web of deception. Indeed, his primary tool today is the sticky web of the Internet, which promises three A's (availability, affordability, and anonymity) to get the man to come back for a second and third glance. By that time, the fourth A (addiction) has all but been assured.

Pornography is an especially serious matter for a husband and a father. First, viewing porn is a direct violation of his marital vows to his wife, to hold her exclusively in his heart in a spousal relationship. You may think, "they're just pictures, not real women," but remember what Jesus said: if a man simply looks at another woman with lust, he commits adultery in his heart (see Mt 5:28). How many online adulterers are there today?

A father should also be mindful of what his porn habit can do to his children. Studies show that eleven is the average age that children encounter porn on the web, and many times the images are found in an online folder that Dad thought was hidden from his kids. Imagine the shame and embarrassment you would feel if your son or daughter found your secret stash or—worse—caught you in the act of viewing porn. Family life is difficult enough without the pain, distortion, and confusion that porn can bring into your life and the lives of your wife and kids. You know, Dad, that you would risk your life to save your loved ones from an intruder. So don't open the door to the insidious danger of porn, and seek to keep your home a place of purity and peace.

Still, you need a plan if you fall. What should a man do once he realizes he is compulsively looking at pornographic images on the Internet or in magazines, and possibly masturbating because of them? The first thing he should do is to humbly and sincerely pray to God for the strength to courageously take back the virtue, the strength, that he has lost to porn. The next step is to go, immediately if possible, to the sacrament of Confession to receive the forgiveness of God.

After a man's soul has been set free from the sin, it is time to implement the following ten steps toward his true freedom from porn and all its attachments:

1. **Admit and resolve.** Every man addicted to porn needs to honestly admit that he doesn't have control over this problem by his own strength. He should resolve to cooperate with God's grace by seeking the necessary support systems and aids in his journey of recovery.

2. **Evaluate home and work environment.** Every porn user should ask if there are any triggers to porn at home or at work. If there are, he should take measures to remove them immediately, including Internet sites and TV shows.

3. **Evaluate friends and social settings.** Each man should assess whether these associations are contributing to his porn use. If so, he should take measures to look for new friends and social settings in his life.

4. **Find patterns.** A man needs to uncover the patterns of his porn use. Often, loneliness is a trigger. He should pursue healthy friendships and relationships that can reduce or eliminate his feelings of frustration and loneliness.

5. **Embrace accountability.** Every recovering porn user needs a group of men for accountability, mentoring, and friendship on his journey toward freedom.

6. **Use prayer power.** Every man should develop a daily prayer life and seek God's forgiveness and grace

whenever he falls to porn. He should avail himself of these graces by praying the Rosary and reading the Bible daily, fasting often, and frequenting the sacraments of Confession (as often as necessary) and the Eucharist (as often as possible).

7. **Find the root sin.** For most porn users it is the deadly sin of pride. To root it out a man should develop the opposing virtue of humility, praying daily to find opportunities to be humble.

8. **Counter temptations with witness**. A man who is seeking freedom from porn should seriously consider taking a stand against the multibillion-dollar porn industry. The King's Men apostolate offers any man this opportunity through the "No More Porn Tour."

9. **Share your story.** A recovering porn addict should prayerfully discern when and where to make a statement about his struggle. This can be done in a men's group or some other forum where trust is met and confidentiality assured.

10. **Set priorities.** For a father, this means placing your wife and children above perceived personal needs. You will die to addiction by living for the good of your family.

These ten steps are by no means the only ways that a man can find healing from porn. Many men will need professional counseling to help them in the process of healing. For some, a good Christian therapist may be a great help in locating the various wounds from a man's past that may be preventing him from finding freedom in his life.

Just as I have experienced personally the destructive effects of porn, I can also now witness to the great freedom and strength that come with breaking the chains of addiction. Probably one of the most distressing effects of porn is that it weakens a man's will, whereas men like to think of themselves as strong. It also distorts the beautiful image of real women in a man's life so that the normal attraction to women—and even to our wives—becomes tainted and soiled.

For most, I pray and believe these steps will be the necessary launching pad for freedom from these sins of the flesh. Isn't this freedom what God wants for us as men made in his image? He wants us to be free to love him and to love others well. But God is a gentleman and asks our cooperation first. All that is needed as you begin your journey is a humble heart and a willing spirit that says to God, "I am ready, please help me."

Conclusion

Three Simple Steps

BRIAN CAULFIELD

At this point in the book you may be thinking, where do I go from here? You know you should probably pray more (chapter 11), show your wife how much you appreciate her (chapter 7), spend more time with the kids (chapter 12), learn more about the faith (chapter 2), find a better balance between work and home life (chapter 3), be more understanding and forgiving (chapter 1), step up and fight the secular culture (chapter 9), and avoid porn (chapter 13), and trust God more (this conclusion) . . . and so on. But you're already overbooked, overstressed, and concerned about far too many things at home and at work.

How could you possibly have time for the "three simple steps" outlined in this final chapter?

1. Pray
2. Love
3. Confess

Are you supposed to change your whole life?

The short answer is yes and no. We all need to change in some ways, and we know that change is challenging and difficult. The good news is that if we take just one small step in the right direction, we will have some powerful help at our side. After all, Jesus said, "If you have faith the size of a mustard seed, you will say to this mountain, 'Move from here to there,' and it will move; and nothing will be impossible for you" (Mt 17:20).

Certainly Jesus didn't mean that one person could change the whole world—or his whole life—all by himself. His point was that if you have just a speck of good will, just a dash of good intention, and you set even one foot in the right direction, God will get you on your way. God will move that mountain. God will change your heart. God will change your whole life. It can happen. God is real, and he wants to show you—even at this very moment—how much he desires to be more a part of your life. He wants to show his love for you.

In a culture that professes to be "spiritual, not religious," many people are not used to thinking in terms of God's personal love for each and every one of us. It's easier to keep God safely distant in the clouds of spirituality rather than let him speak to me here and now about real things going on in my life. But God's love wants to reach into my heart, not in some ideal faraway future time or place, but right here and now in the messiness of my daily life, in the imperfections of my body and soul.

Maybe you're not really comfortable with God's love. After all, lots of guys have trouble with love in their lives, in both expressing it and accepting it.

Maybe God has let you down in the past: you asked for something once, or many times, and didn't get it.

Maybe you don't feel you know God well enough to even talk about him, since you're not on a first-name basis. He's more of a forbidding figure than a personal reality in your life.

Maybe deep down you think you don't deserve God's love because of something you've done or are doing in your life.

Well, join the club. We all feel this way to a greater or lesser degree, and we'd all like to put God aside at one time or another. But God is not put off by any of our excuses, any of our failures, any of our excesses—not even by any of the most secret, embarrassing sins that we commit again and again. Anger, envy, impatience, lying, impurity, adultery—you can go right on through the Ten Commandments. God is not put off. He stands at the door of our hearts, and knocks. What is your response?

You may have noticed that this is not a typical self-help book of ten steps to a happier, healthier, handsomer you. This book is not even like any number of volumes on the popular religion shelf that tell you how to get to God and achieve your dreams. No, this book takes God and you more seriously than that.

This book is not so much about how to reach the goal line as how to get to the starting line. The Christian life is about a series of new beginnings, a succession of new chapters, a progression of new floors that build on one another. The most enduring image of the Christian life is not the victor's crown—though that awaits us—but the pilgrim's palm. At the Second Vatican Council, the image that was chosen for the Church, the body of Christian believers, was the pilgrim who traditionally carries a palm branch in his hand as a sign both of celebration and penitence—remembering when the people of Jerusalem welcomed Jesus by strewing palm fronds at his feet a few days before they called for his crucifixion.

We are on a journey, yet we know that we can never reach the end on our own. The last words of the Bible are not "I did it my way!" but a more humble "Maranatha—Come, Lord Jesus!" Yes, we know that heaven is our goal, but on earth we live the Christian mystery in time. Jesus said on the Cross, "It is finished," yet we've had two-thousand years of human history to think about, respond to, and in many ways obscure that message—the meaning of his life, death, and resurrection. It is evident that God is not yet finished with us, that we are not yet ready to meet him, even as we pray in the Our Father, "Thy Kingdom come."

So what are we to do? We can do nothing good without God, yet we must do something to allow God to work in us. The self-help books have something right—we do need a step-by-step plan from day to day, but we develop it not to "do it my way" but to give God room to work in our lives.

Make your day

The most basic unit of anyone's life is the day. Sun up, sun down. Get up in the morning, earn your daily bread, go to sleep at night. Repeat. If you're going to get things done, or make big or small changes in your life, you have to do it in daily doses.

Our Catholic faith has a lot to teach us in this respect. The official prayer of the Church, called the Divine Office or Liturgy of the Hours, divides the day into periods of prayer. Today we call them Morning Prayer, Daytime Prayer, Evening Prayer, and Night Prayer, but you may have also heard the more traditional Latin names, such as Matins, Lauds, and Terce.

Priests—even those who have busy parish schedules—are required to "pray the hours" each day, reciting the Psalms and reading parts of Scripture, according to a regular cycle. Men and women religious, those in monasteries, set the whole pattern of their days, weeks, years, and lives upon the cycle of prayer prescribed in the Divine Office. If you've ever visited a monastery, you will notice that these individuals who have left the hustle and bustle of the world are still very busy. They typically rise before dawn to pray, attend Mass, and do a portion of their work—all before breakfast. They order their day according to the pattern set centuries ago by St. Benedict—*ora et labora*, pray and work.

Of course, as men with jobs, families, long commutes, hectic schedules, and financial obligations, we are not asked to live the highly structured life of a monk, nor should we try.

We have a different and equally important vocation: to raise and support our families, and seek to shape our worldly affairs according to Gospel values. But to carry out this vital mission, we still need a plan. A daily schedule that is firm yet flexible is a good way to accomplish this.

Make it simple, memorable, and achievable.

The best place to start a new pattern of your life is the morning. Do you hear the alarm, hit the snooze button, lie in bed until the last possible second, drag yourself to the bathroom and kitchen and coffee cup? There's nothing wrong with that, and it may work for you. But if you want to shake up your life, try getting up at the alarm's first ring and saying a little prayer before starting your morning routine. This slight change will make a huge difference in your life. Even if your prayer is as short and simple as "Jesus, please be with me today," God will hear it and you will feel a sense of accomplishment, both spiritually and physically.

From this little act, your whole life can change.

Once you have mastered your morning, take a look at your nighttime routine. After the kids are in bed, maybe you're catching up on work or surfing the Web, or watching TV, or reading a book. If you really want to change your life for the better, turn off the TV or the computer, put down the book ten minutes earlier than usual, and go to a set place in your home to talk to God. Review your day, note any lapses or actual sins, ask God for forgiveness and guidance, and end with a prayer. You have just done an examination of conscience. You may want to have a prayer book handy, but you may also simply recite the three mighty prayers: Our Father, Hail Mary, Glory Be.

Now that you have morning and night, the bookends of your day, in some way directed toward God, it is time to think about the hours in between.

The great Catholic writer G. K. Chesterton was famous for saying, ". . . if a thing is worth doing, it is worth doing badly."[1] Of course, he wasn't suggesting that we set out to fail, or give less than our best effort. He was advising against an attitude that keeps us from trying something unless we know we'll succeed. Another way of expressing it is, "Don't make the perfect the enemy of the good." We probably know someone who wanted to lose weight and set out on the most stringent fad diet for a few weeks before giving into a hot fudge sundae and trashing the whole diet. Or how about those people—maybe you—who are determined to finally get in shape with a new elliptical machine, a new set of weights, a running routine, or a health club membership. Everything goes well for those magic first weeks and then fatigue, sickness, or boredom sets in. There are plenty of dusty exercise machines in basements and unused club memberships strewn across America.

At this point, Chesterton's words are worth considering. Don't strive for perfection from the outset. Set challenging yet reasonable goals that will inspire you, not overburden you. Most of all, don't quit at the first failure. Realize that you are

---

1. G. K. Chesterton, *What's Wrong With the World* (New York: Sheed and Ward, 1956), 192.

weak, breakable, and fallible. Learn to live within your limits even as you slowly push against them. The key concept here is humility—which is not going around saying how awful you are. Humility in the true sense is developing a realistic image of who you are, what you can do, and what you should be doing. A truly humble person can be a great achiever, because he knows his strengths and weaknesses, and is able to build on the strengths while never being discouraged by the weaknesses. We should not really "plan to fail," but we should not be broken in spirit when we fall short.

Three simple steps

Now we get to the "self-help" recipe of the book. Everyone needs a takeaway, a short summary that he can remember and put into practice right away. The many "Seven Secrets" books are appealing because they reduce life to a few bite-size chunks that we can measure. The human heart, mind, and soul long for something better, however, something higher, something real and lasting—ultimately, we seek the eternal. Nothing time-bound will do.

The self-help industry taps into this human longing, but the problem is that its authors set their sights too low. They aim at the horizons of earthly life. To go beyond you need a spiritual—even a specifically Catholic—perspective. That is what I will try to provide here in three simple steps. These are not everything you will need in life, which is much more complex than three steps, but every journey has to start somewhere, and this plan will get you on your way.

Pray. We have already looked briefly at prayer in this chapter, suggesting ways to "bookend" your day with prayer in the morning and at nighttime and by daily examination of conscience. Prayer during the day would be the natural next step, but you should be careful not to strive too soon for perfection. As a family man, you are not called to formal periods of prayer, but you will find it helpful to "keep a line open" to God through brief moments of "recollection," or simply by keeping God in mind.

You may find it surprising that a book about faith and fatherhood would counsel against praying too much, but I have two little stories to illustrate my point.

Raymond Arroyo, a popular host on the Eternal Word Television Network (EWTN) once recalled for me his early days working at the network, when he would keep a regular schedule of visits to the chapel to sit before the Blessed Sacrament and pray. Mother Angelica, the well-known founder of the TV network, told him to cut down on the visits and focus more on his work. He was surprised, but she told him that his "tabernacle" was the work at his desk, computer screen, and the camera that brought his show into millions of homes. As a layman, he needed to move beyond the chapel and find God in the noise and distractions of the world.

The other story involves a man I knew in a prayer group who lamented the breakup of his marriage. In the first years after their wedding, he and his wife had many issues to work out and discuss, but my friend decided that he would go only to God with their problems. As his wife sat lonely and fuming in one room, he would steal away to another room to pray his heart out to God. He realized only after the divorce that he should have communicated with his wife on a human level and listened for God's voice through her legitimate complaints.

As married men, we are called to fit periods of silence and prayer around our primary vocation to wife, family, and work. That will probably mean praying first thing in the morning and at the end of the day, with brief times of "recollection" during the day.

Love. Yes, guys, we need to talk about love. Jesus said that the greatest commandment is to love God with all your heart and your neighbor as yourself. Your closest "neighbors" are your wife and children. Love starts at home.

But take heart, love is not the latest gushy movie or the lyrics to that pop tune you can't get out of your head. True, love has much to do with emotions, and it makes you feel good, but these are not most important, and they don't always last.

The fact is that love—the topic men so often avoid talking about with their buddies or even their wives—is very much a *guy thing*. Don't take my word for it, take God's. The night before he was crucified Jesus said, "No one has greater love than this, to lay down one's life for one's friends" (Jn 15:13).

Love is more about actions than feelings. In fact, love may involve overcoming your emotions. Who, after all, feels like laying down his life? The emotional fear of death must be overcome so that the true nature of love can be revealed.

Action, resolve, toughness, perseverance, sacrifice—these are guy things.

Love involves first of all the will, not the emotions. Another guy thing.

"The experience of a love which involves a real discovery of the other, moving beyond the selfish character that prevailed earlier . . . it seeks the good of the beloved: it becomes renunciation and it is ready, and even willing, for sacrifice."[2]

Love in our culture has been reduced to fleeting emotions or attachments, or to sexual relations in any form. Our culture titillates with talk and images of sexuality, but like sugary treats that give the body a quick lift, they leave us undernourished and craving real food.

Even within our Catholic culture, love and God can be so emotionalized that men can feel like strangers in their own parishes. Though you won't hear it often from the Sunday pulpit, our faith teaches that love is an act of the will. The *Catechism of the Catholic Church* states, "To love is to will the good of another. All other affections have their source in this first movement of the human heart toward the good" (1766).

Love also calls for blood, sweat, and tears—the whole man and everything he can give for his beloved. Love bucks against boundaries, strives for the eternal, jumps the moon, and runs all night to see his loved ones.

So let's make sure we get love right before thinking it's a bunch of empty promises, and get ready to sacrifice a little bit each day in our marriage and family life.

---

2. Benedict XVI, Deus Caritas Est (Boston: Pauline Books & Media, 2005), no. 6.

Confess. If you are Catholic, you are a Christian doubly blessed because of the sacraments. Maybe you already know this. Or maybe you feel a bit embarrassed being Catholic these days, with all the horrible revelations about some priests, or the charge that Catholicism is against sex, science, and the modern world. Wherever you are in your walk of faith, you may be interested in my personal conversion story.

I was raised Catholic, went to Catholic schools in New York from kindergarten to college, yet in my teens I fell away from the faith. I stopped going to Mass, started reading skeptics like Nietzsche and Ayn Rand, and thought myself somewhat smart. For ten years, I went through the big changes in my life—college, first job, my own apartment—without much thought of God or the Church. I was happy enough, but something was missing.

One day I stopped into a church on the way home and was surprised to see a weekday evening Mass attended by so many people. A deep sense that I was missing something overcame me and my eye was drawn to the red vigil light that I knew marked the tabernacle, where Jesus was present in the Blessed Sacrament. I felt a gentle movement of my heart that told me I needed to come back. So I did, time and again after work, sitting in the back of the church, afraid to be seen or to go forward for Communion, but listening to the readings and recalling the familiar flow of the Mass. Then I noticed another little red light: this one over the confessional box. People were going in and out and I knew my life was suddenly at a very painful turning point. Should I go to Confession? Maybe. Yes. No. I chickened out that day and many days to follow. But eventually I found courage, made a list of the more obvious sins over the past ten years, and got in the Confession line, sure that everyone in the church was looking at me and shouting in their minds, "Sinner!"

I felt a huge sense of strangeness and relief after confessing and was glad to be able to receive Communion again. But let's face it, guys, sexual sins such as pornography, masturbation, and impure thoughts are not easily overcome. I needed to go to Confession a lot, and receive Communion often, to even begin on the right road.

So step three is—if you haven't been to Confession in a while, pick a church, find a time, and go. Sure you're scared, weak, and sinful, but go. Then consider the fact that Jesus is really, truly present in Holy Communion—his body, blood, soul, and divinity—and realize that if you were the only person on earth he still would go through the crucifixion for your soul. Receive Jesus with these thoughts, and know that he will be with you always.

As you go forward with your life as a husband and father, you will face many challenges and heartbreaks, and hopefully experience your share of joys. Your life will not always be easy and may even be marked by hardship. But if you are a father of faith, you will be blessed, and your wife and children will be as well.

Acknowledgments

The Cub Scout motto "Do your best," trademark ᵀᴹ 2013, Boy Scouts of America.

Any other trademarked designations that appear in this book are used in good faith but are not authorized by, associated with, or sponsored by the trademark owners.

Excerpts from the English translation of *Rite of Marriage* © 1969, International Commission on English in the Liturgy Corporation. All rights reserved.

Excerpts from *Millennials: A Portrait of Generation Next* © 2010, Pew Research Center, Social & Demographic Trends Project. http://www.pewsocialtrends.org/files/2010/10/millennials-confident-connected-open-to-change.pdf. Used with permission.

Excerpts from *For Millennials, Parenthood Trumps Marriage* © 2011, Pew Research Center, Social & Demographic Trends Project. http://www.pew socialtrends.org/files/2011/03/millennials-marriage.pdf. Used with permission.

Excerpts from G. K. Chesterton, *What's Wrong With the World* (New York: Sheed and Ward, 1956). Used with permission of A P Watt Ltd. on behalf of The Royal Literary Fund.

Excerpts from *A Civilization of Love* by Carl Anderson. Copyright © 2008, Knights of Columbus. Reprinted courtesy of HarperCollins Publishers.

Excerpts used with permission from © Libreria Editrice Vaticana, Vatican City:

Excerpts from the English translation of the *Catechism of the Catholic Church* for use in the United States of America, copyright © 1994, United States Catholic Conference, Inc.

Pope John Paul II, *Mulieris Dignitatem*, © 1988.

Pope John Paul II, *Letter to Families*, © 1994.

Pope John Paul II, *Man and Woman He Created Them: A Theology of the Body*, © 1986, 2006.

Pope John Paul II, *Laetamur Magnopere*, © 1997.

Pope Benedict XVI, *Letter of His Holiness Benedict XVI to the Participants in the Fifth World Meeting of Families*, © 2005.

Pope Benedict XVI, *Jesus of Nazareth, Part Two: Holy Week from the Entrance into Jerusalem to the Resurrection*, © 2011.

About the Authors

Mike Aquilina has been married to Terri for twenty-seven years, and together they have six children. He is author or editor of more than forty books on Catholic history, doctrine, and devotion. His website is mikeaquilina.com.

Deacon Harold Burke-Sivers is president and chief executive of Servant Enterprises Inc., a Catholic evangelization and apologetics organization. He and his wife, Colleen, have four children.

Brian Caulfield is the editor of the website Fathers for Good (fathersforgood.org), sponsored by the Knights of Columbus, and edits the weekly "Catholic Men" column for the Catholic News Agency's website.

Bill Donaghy is a speaker with the Theology of the Body Institute, and teaches theology at a Catholic high school in

Pennsylvania. He and his wife, Rebecca, live in Lansdowne, Pennsylvania, with their two young children.

Jonathan Doyle, a husband, father, and businessman, is founder of Choicez Media and beingCatholic.com.au. He speaks to thousands of people each year on issues related to manhood and sexuality. He holds a master's degree in education and is completing further postgraduate study at the Pontifical John Paul II Institute for Studies on Marriage and the Family at The Catholic University of America.

Jason Godin teaches U.S. history at Blinn College in Bryan, Texas, where he lives with his wife and two children. He is a contributor to the "Catholic Men" column for the Catholic News Agency.

Raymond N. Guarendi, Ph.D., is a practicing clinical psychologist who specializes in parenting and behavioral issues. He has written five books on these topics, hosts a Catholic call-in show, and shares his thoughts at drray.com. He and his wife, Randi, are parents to ten children whom they adopted.

Mark Houck is the co-founder and president of The King's Men (thekingsmen.org) and the Founder of the Samson Healing Retreat for Men (samsonretreat.com). He and his wife, Ryan-Marie, have three children.

Peter C. Kleponis, Ph.D., is a licensed clinical therapist and assistant director of Comprehensive Counseling Services in

West Conshohocken, Pennsylvania, specializing in marriage and family therapy. He is certified in the diagnosis and treatment of sexual addictions, and provides resources at integri tyrestored.com. He and his wife, Maria, have a young son.

Gerald Korson is a freelance book editor and journalist, and former editor of *Our Sunday Visitor*, a weekly Catholic newspaper. He and his wife, Christina, have eleven children.

Patrick Madrid is the director of the Envoy Institute and author of eighteen books on Catholic living and evangelization. He hosts a daily Catholic radio show called *Right Here, Right Now*. He and his wife, Nancy, have eleven children who all practice the Catholic faith.

Damon C. Owens is the executive director of the Theology of the Body Institute (tobinstitute.org) and speaks widely about marriage and family life. Married to Melanie, he is the father of seven daughters and one son.

Rick Sarkisian, Ph.D., the father of five children, is an author and speaker on vocations, life purpose, authentic manhood, and St. Joseph. His website is lifeworkpress.com.

BOOKS & MEDIA

The Daughters of St. Paul operate book and media centers at the following addresses. Visit, call, or write the one nearest you today, or find us at www.pauline.org

CALIFORNIA

3908 Sepulveda Blvd, Culver City, CA 90230	310-397-8676
935 Brewster Avenue, Redwood City, CA 94063	650-369-4230
5945 Balboa Avenue, San Diego, CA 92111	858-565-9181

FLORIDA

145 S.W. 107th Avenue, Miami, FL 33174	305-559-6715

HAWAII

1143 Bishop Street, Honolulu, HI 96813	808-521-2731
Neighbor Islands call:	866-521-2731

ILLINOIS

172 North Michigan Avenue, Chicago, IL 60601	312-346-4228

LOUISIANA

4403 Veterans Memorial Blvd, Metairie, LA 70006	504-887-7631

MASSACHUSETTS

885 Providence Hwy, Dedham, MA 02026	781-326-5385

MISSOURI

9804 Watson Road, St. Louis, MO 63126	314-965-3512

NEW YORK

64 W. 38th Street, New York, NY 10018	212-754-1110

PENNSYLVANIA

Philadelphia—relocating	215-676-9494

SOUTH CAROLINA

243 King Street, Charleston, SC 29401	843-577-0175

VIRGINIA

1025 King Street, Alexandria, VA 22314	703-549-3806

CANADA

3022 Dufferin Street, Toronto, ON M6B 3T5	416-781-9131

¡También somos su fuente para libros,
videos y música en español!